# THIS BOOK

## BELONGS TO

..................................................................

..................................................................

**Thanks ever so much to each of my cherished readers for investing the time to read this book!**

I know you could have picked from many other books, but you chose this one. So, a big thanks for reading all the way to the end. If you enjoyed this book or received value from it, I'd like to ask you for a favor. Please take a few minutes to **post an honest and heartfelt review on** Amazon.com. Your support does make a difference and helps to benefit other people.

*Thanks!*

# Table of Contents

# SUMMARY

**What is the Delicate World of Bobbin Lace?:** The delicate world of bobbin lace is a fascinating and intricate craft that has been practiced for centuries. It involves the weaving of threads on a pillow using bobbins and pins to create intricate lace patterns. This traditional form of lace-making requires great skill, patience, and attention to detail.

Bobbin lace originated in Europe in the 16th century and quickly gained popularity among the nobility and upper classes. It was considered a highly prestigious skill and was often used to adorn clothing, accessories, and home decor. The delicate and intricate patterns created with bobbin lace were seen as a symbol of wealth and status.

The process of creating bobbin lace begins with a pattern, which is usually drawn on a piece of parchment or pricked onto a card. The pattern serves as a guide for the lace-maker and determines the design and shape of the lace. The lace-maker then sets up their pillow, which is a cushioned surface on which the lace is created.

The lace-maker uses pairs of bobbins, which are small wooden or plastic spools, to hold the threads. Each pair of bobbins holds a different thread, and the lace-maker manipulates the threads by crossing them over each other in a specific sequence. The pins are used to secure the threads in place on the pillow, allowing the lace-maker to work on different sections of the pattern at a time.

The process of creating bobbin lace is slow and meticulous. The lace-maker must carefully manipulate the threads, ensuring that they are crossed over each other in the correct order and tension. Mistakes can easily be made, and undoing and redoing sections of the lace is a common occurrence. This requires great patience and attention to detail.

As the lace progresses, the lace-maker may need to add or remove bobbins to accommodate the changing pattern. This requires careful planning and organization to ensure that the threads are kept in the correct order and tension. The lace-maker must also constantly refer to the pattern to ensure that they are following it correctly and creating the desired design.

Once the lace is complete, it is removed from the pillow and carefully finished. This may involve trimming excess threads, securing loose ends, and blocking the lace to shape it properly. The finished lace can then be used for a variety of purposes, such as clothing embellishments, table linens, or decorative pieces.

**Celebrating the Intricacy and Elegance of Lace-Making of Bobbin Lace**: The art of bobbin lace-making is a time-honored tradition that has captivated artisans and enthusiasts for centuries. This intricate and elegant craft involves weaving delicate threads together using a series of bobbins, resulting in stunning lace patterns that are both visually stunning and incredibly detailed.

The origins of bobbin lace-making can be traced back to the 16th century, where it first emerged in Europe as a popular pastime for noblewomen. However, it quickly gained popularity among all social classes, as the demand for lace grew and the techniques became more refined. Bobbin lace-making soon became a highly sought-after skill, with artisans dedicating countless hours to perfecting their craft.

The process of creating bobbin lace is a meticulous one, requiring a steady hand and a keen eye for detail. It begins with a pattern, which is often drawn on a piece of parchment or pricked onto a cushion. The lace-maker then carefully winds threads onto bobbins, each one representing a different element of the pattern. These bobbins are then manipulated and crossed over each other in a precise manner, creating the intricate lacework.

One of the most fascinating aspects of bobbin lace-making is the variety of stitches and techniques that can be employed. From simple braids and twists to more complex patterns such as spiders and flowers, the possibilities are endless. Each stitch requires a different combination of movements, and the lace-maker must carefully follow the pattern to ensure the desired outcome.

The materials used in bobbin lace-making are also of great importance. Traditionally, fine linen or silk threads were used, as they provided the necessary strength and delicacy required for the craft. Today, however, lace-makers have a wide range of materials at their disposal, including metallic threads, synthetic fibers, and even beads and sequins, allowing for even more creativity and experimentation.

The end result of bobbin lace-making is a true work of art. The intricate patterns and delicate details of the lace are a testament to the skill and dedication of the artisan. From delicate lace collars and cuffs to elaborate tablecloths and curtains, bobbin lace can be found in a variety of applications, both functional and decorative.

In recent years, there has been a resurgence of interest in bobbin lace-making, with workshops and classes being offered to those eager to learn this ancient craft.

**Navigating Through This Comprehensive Guide of Bobbin Lace:**
Welcome to this comprehensive guide on navigating through the world of bobbin lace! Whether you are a beginner or an experienced lace maker, this guide aims to provide you with all the information you need to master this intricate and beautiful craft.

Bobbin lace is a traditional form of lace making that involves weaving threads together using bobbins and pins. It is a technique that has been practiced for centuries and has evolved into various styles and patterns across different cultures. This guide will take you through the basics of bobbin lace, including the tools and materials you will need to get started.

First and foremost, let's talk about the essential tools for bobbin lace making. You will need bobbins, which are small spools that hold the threads, and pins, which are used to secure the lace as you work. There are different types of bobbins available, such as wooden bobbins, bone bobbins, and plastic bobbins, each with its own advantages and disadvantages. It is important to choose the type of bobbin that feels comfortable in your hands and suits your personal preferences.

Next, let's discuss the threads used in bobbin lace making. Traditionally, linen thread was used, but nowadays, you can find a variety of threads in different colors and thicknesses. The choice of thread will depend on the type of lace you want to create and the desired effect. It is recommended to start with a medium-weight thread for beginners, as it is easier to handle and manipulate.

Once you have gathered your tools and materials, it's time to learn the basic stitches and techniques of bobbin lace making. The most common stitches include the half stitch, whole stitch, and twisted stitch. These stitches are combined in various ways to create different patterns and designs. It is important to practice these stitches until you feel comfortable and confident in executing them accurately.

As you progress in your bobbin lace making journey, you can explore more advanced techniques and patterns. There are countless books, online resources, and workshops available that can help you expand your skills and knowledge. It is also beneficial to join a lace making group or community, where you can connect with fellow lace makers, share ideas, and learn from each other's experiences.

In addition to the technical aspects of bobbin lace making, it is important to consider the design and aesthetics of your lace. You can experiment with different patterns, colors, and textures to create unique and personalized pieces.

**The Origins and Evolution of Bobbin Lace:** The origins and evolution of bobbin lace can be traced back to the 16th century in Europe. It is believed to have originated in Italy, where it was initially known as "punto in aria" or "stitch in the air". The technique of bobbin lace-making quickly spread throughout Europe, becoming particularly popular in countries such as Belgium, France, and England.

Bobbin lace is a delicate and intricate form of lace-making that involves weaving threads together using a series of bobbins. The bobbins are wound with thread and manipulated to create various patterns and designs. The lace is made by crossing and twisting the threads over a pattern, which is usually pinned to a pillow or cushion.

In the early days of bobbin lace-making, the patterns were simple and geometric, often consisting of straight lines and basic shapes. However, as the technique evolved and became more popular, lace-makers began to experiment with more complex designs, incorporating flowers, animals, and even human figures into their work.

During the 17th and 18th centuries, bobbin lace-making reached its peak in popularity. It became a highly sought-after skill, and lace-makers were often commissioned to create intricate lace pieces for the nobility and upper classes. The lace was used to adorn clothing, accessories, and even furniture.

In the 19th century, the industrial revolution brought about significant changes in the production of lace. Machines were invented that could produce lace more quickly and efficiently than by hand. This led to a decline in the demand for handmade bobbin lace, as machine-made lace became more affordable and accessible.

However, bobbin lace-making did not disappear entirely. It continued to be practiced by a dedicated group of artisans and enthusiasts who valued the traditional craftsmanship and intricate beauty of handmade lace. Today, bobbin lace-making is considered a niche craft, with dedicated communities and organizations that promote and preserve the art form.

In recent years, there has been a resurgence of interest in bobbin lace-making, as people seek out unique and handmade items in a world dominated by mass-produced goods. The craft has also benefited from advancements in technology, with the internet providing a platform for lace-makers to connect, share patterns, and showcase their work to a global audience.

The origins and evolution of bobbin lace are a testament to the enduring appeal of this intricate and delicate craft.

**Cultural and Artistic Significance of Bobbin Lace**: The cultural and artistic significance of bobbin lace cannot be overstated. This intricate and delicate craft has a rich history that spans centuries and has been cherished by cultures around the world.

Bobbin lace, also known as pillow lace, is a technique that involves weaving threads together using bobbins and a pillow. The process requires great skill and precision, as the lace is created by carefully twisting and crossing the threads to form intricate patterns and designs. This meticulous craftsmanship has made bobbin lace a highly valued art form.

One of the most significant aspects of bobbin lace is its cultural significance. Throughout history, lace has been associated with wealth, luxury, and nobility. In many cultures, lace was a symbol of status and was often used to adorn clothing, accessories, and even furniture. The production and wearing of lace became a way for individuals to display their wealth and social standing.

Bobbin lace also played a significant role in the economy of many regions. In the 16th and 17th centuries, lace production became a major industry in Europe, particularly in countries such as Belgium, France, and Italy. Lace-making guilds were established, and lace became a valuable export commodity. The lace industry provided employment opportunities for many women, who would often work from home to create intricate lace pieces.

Beyond its economic and cultural significance, bobbin lace is also highly regarded for its artistic value. The intricate patterns and delicate designs created through this technique are truly awe-inspiring. Lace-makers would often incorporate various motifs and symbols into their designs, such as flowers, animals, and geometric shapes. These designs were not only visually appealing but also carried symbolic meanings, reflecting the cultural and social values of the time.

Bobbin lace has also been used as a form of artistic expression. Many lace-makers would create elaborate lace pieces that were not intended for practical use but rather as works of art. These lace artworks would often be displayed in museums and galleries, showcasing the skill and creativity of the lace-maker.

In recent years, bobbin lace has experienced a resurgence in popularity. While the craft was at risk of dying out in the 20th century, there has been a renewed interest in preserving and promoting this traditional art form. Lace-making schools and workshops have been established, allowing individuals to learn the techniques and skills required to create bobbin lace. Additionally, contemporary lace-makers have been pushing the boundaries of the craft, experimenting with new materials and techniques to create innovative and unique lace designs.

**Modern-Day Bobbin Lace Making**: Modern-day bobbin lace making is a traditional craft that has evolved and adapted to the contemporary world. It involves the intricate weaving of threads using bobbins and a pillow, resulting in delicate and intricate lace patterns. This art form has a rich history dating back centuries, but it has also embraced modern techniques and materials to keep up with the times.

In the past, bobbin lace making was primarily done by hand, with skilled artisans meticulously weaving threads together to create intricate lace designs. However, with the advent of technology, modern-day bobbin lace makers have access to a wide range of tools and equipment that make the process more efficient and precise.

One of the key advancements in modern bobbin lace making is the use of computer-aided design (CAD) software. This technology allows lace makers to create intricate lace patterns digitally, which can then be translated into a physical design. This not only saves time but also allows for more complex and detailed designs to be created.

Another innovation in modern bobbin lace making is the use of synthetic threads. Traditionally, lace was made using natural fibers such as linen or silk. However, modern lace makers have the option to use synthetic threads, which offer a wider range of colors and textures. These threads are also more durable and easier to work with, making the lace making process more accessible to beginners.

Additionally, modern bobbin lace makers have access to a wide range of specialized tools and equipment. These include specialized bobbins, pillows, and pins, which are designed to make the lace making process more efficient and precise. For example, modern bobbins are often made from lightweight materials such as plastic or carbon fiber, which reduces fatigue and allows for faster weaving.

Furthermore, the internet has played a significant role in the modernization of bobbin lace making. Online communities and forums allow lace makers from around the world to connect and share their knowledge and techniques. This has created a global network of lace makers who can learn from each other and collaborate on projects.

In conclusion, modern-day bobbin lace making is a craft that has embraced technology and innovation while still honoring its traditional roots. With advancements in CAD software, the use of synthetic threads, specialized tools, and the power of online communities, bobbin lace makers have more resources than ever before to create intricate and beautiful lace designs. This art form continues to evolve and adapt, ensuring its relevance and popularity in the contemporary world.

**Essential Tools and Materials of Bobbin Lace**: Bobbin lace is a delicate and intricate form of lace-making that requires a specific set of tools and materials to create beautiful and intricate designs. These tools and materials are essential for any bobbin lace enthusiast to have in order to successfully create their own lace pieces.

One of the most important tools in bobbin lace-making is the pillow. The pillow is a soft and cushioned surface that provides a stable and comfortable base for working on the lace. It is usually made of foam or a similar material and comes in various sizes and shapes to accommodate different lace-making techniques. The pillow is where the lace pattern is pinned and secured, allowing the lace-maker to work on the design with ease and precision.

Another essential tool in bobbin lace-making is the bobbins. Bobbins are small spools or cylinders that hold the thread used in creating the lace. They are typically made of wood or plastic and come in different sizes and shapes. The number of bobbins used depends on the complexity of the lace pattern, with more intricate designs requiring a larger number of bobbins. The bobbins are used to manipulate the threads and create the various stitches and patterns that make up the lace.

In addition to the pillow and bobbins, other tools that are necessary for bobbin lace-making include pins, needles, and thread. Pins are used to secure the lace pattern to the pillow and keep it in place while working on it. Needles are used to sew the lace together and create the intricate details and connections between the threads. Thread, on the other hand, is the material used to create the lace itself. It can be made of various materials such as cotton, silk, or linen, and comes in different thicknesses and colors to achieve different effects and designs.

Apart from the tools, there are also specific materials that are essential for bobbin lace-making. These include patterns, which are the guides or templates that lace-makers follow to create their designs. Patterns can be purchased or created by the lace-maker themselves, and they provide the instructions and diagrams for creating the lace. Lace-makers also need a variety of threads in different colors to achieve the desired look and effect in their lace pieces. Additionally, lace-makers may use embellishments such as beads or sequins to add extra detail and sparkle to their lace creations.

In conclusion, bobbin lace-making requires a specific set of tools and materials to create intricate and beautiful lace designs.

**Setting Up Your Lace-Making Space of Bobbin Lace**: Setting up your lace-making space for bobbin lace requires careful planning and organization to ensure a comfortable and efficient working environment. Here are some detailed steps to help you create the perfect lace-making space:

1. Choose a suitable location: Select a well-lit area in your home where you can set up your lace-making space. Natural light is ideal, but if that's not possible, make sure you have adequate artificial lighting.

2. Consider the size of your workspace: Determine how much space you need based on the size of your projects and the number of bobbins you typically work with. Ensure that you have enough room to spread out your lace pillow and have easy access to your supplies.

3. Select a sturdy table or desk: Look for a table or desk that is stable and provides a comfortable working height. Avoid using a surface that is too high or too low, as it can strain your back and neck.

4. Invest in a quality lace pillow: Choose a lace pillow that suits your needs and preferences. There are various types available, such as round, rectangular, or bolster pillows. Consider the size and firmness of the pillow, as well as any additional features like a cover or storage compartments.

5. Organize your bobbins: Bobbins are an essential tool in bobbin lace-making, so it's important to keep them organized. Use a bobbin rack or bobbin tree to store your bobbins neatly and prevent them from tangling. You can also label your bobbins with thread colors or patterns to easily identify them during your projects.

6. Arrange your supplies: Keep all your lace-making supplies within reach. This includes pins, thread, scissors, and any other tools you use regularly. Consider using small containers or trays to keep your supplies organized and easily accessible.

7. Create a comfortable seating arrangement: Since lace-making can be a time-consuming activity, it's crucial to have a comfortable chair or stool. Look for a seat that provides good back support and allows you to maintain a proper posture while working.

8. Ensure proper ventilation: Lace-making can generate dust and fibers, so it's important to have proper ventilation in your lace-making space. Open windows or use a fan to circulate fresh air and prevent any respiratory discomfort.

9. Personalize your space: Make your lace-making space your own by adding personal touches. Hang up inspirational quotes, display finished lace pieces, or incorporate decorative elements that inspire your creativity.

**Basic Stitches and Techniques of Bobbin Lace:** Bobbin lace is a delicate and intricate form of lace-making that involves weaving threads together using a series of bobbins. This traditional craft dates back centuries and has been passed down through generations, resulting in a wide variety of stitches and techniques that can be used to create stunning lace designs.

One of the most basic stitches in bobbin lace is the half stitch. This stitch is created by crossing two pairs of threads over each other in an X shape. The pairs of threads are then twisted around each other, creating a secure and tight stitch. The half stitch is often used as a foundation for more complex stitches and patterns in bobbin lace.

Another commonly used stitch in bobbin lace is the whole stitch. This stitch is similar to the half stitch, but instead of crossing two pairs of threads, four pairs of threads are crossed over each other in a square shape. The pairs of threads are then twisted around each other, creating a larger and more decorative stitch. The whole stitch can be used to create intricate patterns and designs in bobbin lace.

In addition to these basic stitches, there are also various techniques that can be used in bobbin lace. One such technique is called "gimping". Gimping involves adding a thicker thread, known as a gimp, to the lace design. The gimp is woven in and out of the stitches, creating a raised and textured effect. This technique is often used to add dimension and interest to bobbin lace designs.

Another technique commonly used in bobbin lace is called "grounding." Grounding involves creating a solid background for the lace design. This is done by weaving a series of threads in a specific pattern, creating a solid base for the lace stitches to be worked on. Grounding can be done in a variety of patterns and can greatly enhance the overall appearance of the lace design.

Bobbin lace also incorporates various decorative techniques, such as picots and tallies. Picots are small loops that are created by twisting the thread around a pin or needle. These loops can be used to create decorative edges or to add interest to the lace design. Tallies, on the other hand, are small bars or lines that are created by twisting the thread in a specific way. These bars can be used to create intricate patterns and designs within the lace.

Overall, the basic stitches and techniques of bobbin lace provide a foundation for creating beautiful and intricate lace designs.

## Resolving Common Lace-Making Issues of Bobbin Lace:

Bobbin lace-making is a delicate and intricate craft that requires precision and attention to detail. However, even the most experienced lace-makers can encounter common issues that can hinder their progress and result in less-than-perfect lacework. In this article, we will explore some of these common issues and provide tips and techniques to resolve them.

One common issue that lace-makers often face is tension problems. Maintaining consistent tension throughout the lace-making process is crucial for achieving uniform and balanced lace. Uneven tension can lead to loose or tight areas in the lace, which can be visually unappealing. To resolve this issue, it is important to regularly check and adjust the tension of the bobbins. This can be done by gently pulling on the threads to ensure they are all equally taut. Additionally, using a tensioning device, such as a pillow or a lace-making stand, can help maintain consistent tension throughout the lace-making process.

Another common issue in bobbin lace-making is making mistakes or errors in the pattern. Lace patterns can be complex and intricate, and it is not uncommon for lace-makers to make mistakes while following the pattern. To resolve this issue, it is important to have a good understanding of the pattern before starting the lace-making process. Taking the time to carefully read and analyze the pattern can help identify potential areas of confusion or difficulty. Additionally, using markers or pins to highlight key points in the pattern can help prevent mistakes and ensure accurate lacework.

Thread breakage is another common issue that lace-makers often encounter. This can be frustrating and time-consuming, especially when working with delicate and fine threads. To resolve this issue, it is important to use high-quality threads that are strong and durable. Additionally, regularly checking the tension of the threads and ensuring they are not too tight can help prevent breakage. If a thread does break, it is important to carefully reattach it to the bobbins and continue the lace-making process without compromising the overall integrity of the lace.

Lastly, lace-makers often struggle with maintaining focus and concentration during the lace-making process. Bobbin lace-making requires a high level of concentration and attention to detail, and distractions can easily lead to mistakes or errors. To resolve this issue, it is important to create a dedicated and quiet workspace where distractions can be minimized. Additionally, taking regular breaks and practicing mindfulness techniques, such as deep breathing or meditation, can help improve focus and concentration during the lace making.

**Tips for Efficient and Enjoyable Lace Making of Bobbin Lace:**

Bobbin lace making is a beautiful and intricate craft that requires patience, precision, and attention to detail. Whether you are a beginner or an experienced lace maker, there are several tips that can help you make your lace making process more efficient and enjoyable.

1. Choose the Right Tools: Having the right tools is essential for efficient lace making. Invest in good quality bobbins, pins, and a sturdy lace pillow. Make sure your bobbins are lightweight and smooth to prevent any unnecessary strain on your hands. Additionally, having a well-padded lace pillow will provide a comfortable and stable surface for your lace making.

2. Organize Your Threads: Before you start your lace making project, take the time to organize your threads. Sort them by color and type, and wind them onto separate bobbins. This will make it easier for you to find the thread you need and prevent any tangling or confusion during the lace making process.

3. Practice Proper Tension: Maintaining proper tension is crucial for creating even and well-defined lace patterns. Avoid pulling your threads too tightly or leaving them too loose. Practice finding the right balance by experimenting with different tensions until you achieve the desired result. Remember, consistent tension throughout your lace making project will ensure a professional-looking finished product.

4. Start with Simple Patterns: If you are new to bobbin lace making, it is advisable to start with simple patterns. This will help you build your skills and confidence before attempting more complex designs. Begin with basic stitches and gradually progress to more intricate patterns as you become more comfortable with the technique.

5. Take Breaks: Lace making can be a time-consuming process that requires a lot of concentration. It is important to take regular breaks to rest your hands and eyes. This will prevent fatigue and allow you to maintain focus and precision throughout your lace making session. Stretching your hands and doing simple exercises can also help prevent any strain or discomfort.

6. Join a Lace Making Group: Joining a lace making group or attending workshops can be a great way to enhance your skills and meet fellow lace makers. These groups provide a supportive and inspiring environment where you can learn new techniques, exchange ideas, and

gain valuable insights from experienced lace makers. Additionally, being part of a community of lace makers can make the process more enjoyable and rewarding.

**Enhancing Your Lace-Making Skills of Bobbin Lace:** If you are looking to enhance your lace-making skills in the art of bobbin lace, you have come to the right place. Bobbin lace is a delicate and intricate craft that involves weaving threads together using bobbins to create beautiful lace patterns. Whether you are a beginner or have some experience in bobbin lace-making, there are several ways you can improve your skills and take your craft to the next level.

First and foremost, it is important to have a solid understanding of the basic techniques and stitches used in bobbin lace-making. This includes learning how to make a variety of stitches such as the half stitch, whole stitch, and twisted stitch. Familiarize yourself with the different types of bobbins and their functions, as well as the various types of threads and their properties. Understanding these fundamentals will provide a strong foundation for your lace-making journey.

Once you have mastered the basics, it is time to challenge yourself with more complex patterns and designs. Start by selecting patterns that are slightly more advanced than what you are comfortable with. This will push you to learn new techniques and stitches, and expand your repertoire of lace-making skills. Look for patterns that incorporate different types of grounds, fillings, and decorative elements. Experiment with different thread combinations and colors to add depth and dimension to your lace.

In addition to practicing patterns, it is also beneficial to join a lace-making group or attend workshops and classes. Connecting with other lace-makers will not only provide you with a supportive community, but also expose you to different styles and techniques. Sharing ideas and experiences with fellow lace-makers can inspire you to try new things and improve your skills. Workshops and classes led by experienced lace-makers can offer valuable guidance and feedback, helping you refine your techniques and troubleshoot any challenges you may encounter.

Another way to enhance your lace-making skills is to study the history and traditions of bobbin lace. Understanding the origins and cultural significance of this craft can deepen your appreciation for it and inspire you to create lace that reflects its rich heritage. Research different lace-making traditions from around the world and explore the work of renowned lace-makers throughout history. This knowledge can inform your own designs and help you develop a unique style.

Lastly, don't be afraid to experiment and think outside the box. While it is important to learn and follow traditional techniques, don't be afraid to add your own creative twist to your lace-making.

# Introduction

This book describes various ways you can use colour within Torchon bobbin lace. Why use colour? Because it's fun, easy, and something new to try. A simple, even dull, pattern becomes interesting with a bit of colour. But it goes beyond that. Colour shows you how threads move through the lace. A lacemaker is usually aware of this, but colour allows the onlooker to see it as well.

This book won't teach you how to make bobbin lace. See my book "How to make Bobbin Lace" for that. But the patterns are simple and most only use a few pairs, so it is suitable for lacemaking beginners.

This book covers Torchon lace. Other lace styles can use colour, but Torchon lace is geometric, with dependable directions of thread. This makes it particularly interesting to explore colour.

It is tricky to use a pattern in an e-book! Even a paperback may have the pattern in the wrong size for you. So all the patterns in this book (and instructions on how to change the pattern size) are available here:

# Patterns

## Torchon ground and double Torchon ground

Torchon ground is the net or ground mostly used in Torchon net. It is very simple, but you can produce interesting effects in colour, especially if you combine it with double Torchon ground.

The following patterns are insertions, or pieces of lace with two straight edges. Headsides produce complications, which this book covers later.

Insertions can be used to decorate clothes. Normally we sew lace onto the
edge of a piece of material. However, if we sew the lace onto the material instead, the colour of the material shows through the lace. Insertions can make very pretty decorative borders, for example on a sleeve at the wrist.

You may need to make a piece longer than your lace pillow. There are other types of lace pillow which let you do this, such as a block pillow, a roller pillow or a bolster.

There are a lot of different patterns in this book. I don't expect you work them all. Flip through the patterns until you find one you like. However, you might find it useful to read through the section to understand the techniques involved. The patterns give colours, but choose your own colours if you wish.

## Pattern 1a - Basic Torchon ground

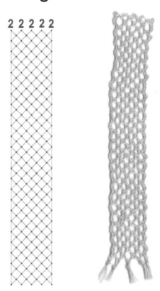

2 2 2 2 2

This is the basis for the next few patterns. It is a piece of Torchon ground with a Winkie pin footside or edge. It uses 10 pairs.

This is a Torchon ground stitch. You can see that the pairs swap

over.

A normal footside swaps over the pair from the lace and the edge pair.

However, this lace will have a Winkie pin footside. The pair from the lace works through the passive pair, goes round the pin, and back through the passive pair to return to the lace immediately.

It doesn't really matter how the pairs travel through the lace, since they are all the same colour. See what happens in the next few patterns, once we start to introduce colour.

This is a very boring piece of lace! You don't need to work it as long as you understand it. If you do want to work it, then it is only necessary to work a few rows.

# **Pattern 1b -** Simple zigzag

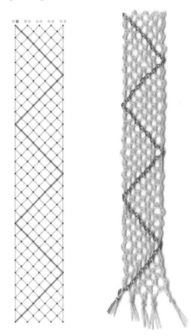

This is exactly the same piece of lace as pattern 1a (basic Torchon ground), but one pair has been wound with a different colour. I've put blobs of colour at the start of the pattern to show which colour starts where.

You work the coloured pair exactly the same as the others – Torchon ground and Winkie pin footside. You can see the effect!

This is not, perhaps, an exciting pattern. It is demonstrating the principle of using colour.

You can try making the coloured pair start on a different pin. The effect will be much the same, starting in a different place. However, if you make either of the pairs at the extreme edge coloured, the colour stays at the edge. The edge pairs are passives.

# Pattern 1c - Simple diamonds

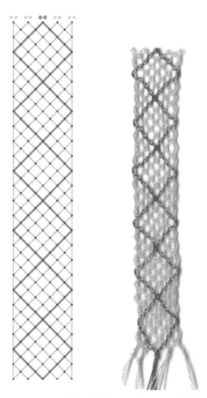

Here, we have two pairs wound with colour. They both start in the middle, and move in different directions. It gives a diamond effect.

The working is exactly the same as the previous few patterns.

**Tip**: If you have spangled bobbins, or bobbins that you can identify in some way, then look out two special pairs and make them the edge pairs. Remember (from the last pattern) that the edge pairs should stay at the edge because they are passives. That means that you can double check after the stitch at the edge to make sure that the special pair is still at the edge. Yes, I know that a lacemaker should be able to make lace without such simple checks. But we all make mistakes, don't we?

The other pairs travel throughout the lace (this is what we are exploring, after all), but the bobbins within a pair should stay together. So you can check that, as well.

## Pattern 1d - Double zigzag

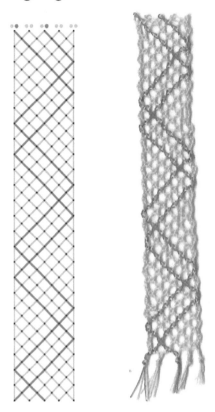

There are still two pairs wound with a different colour to the rest, but now they start on different starting pins. The rest of the pattern remains the same.

I mentioned pattern 1b that it didn't really matter where the coloured pair started, as long as the passives of the footside weren't coloured. Once you get more than one pair, it does matter. In pattern 1c, the two pairs started in the middle. Here, one starts in the middle, and the other on an edge pin (but not at the edge).

You could try starting on other pins to see what happens. Print off pattern 1a (basic Torchon ground), and draw on it some straight lines, starting at the top, going diagonally, and bouncing off the edge when it reaches one. If you find that you have made an attractive pattern, then try it out. You have just designed an original piece of lace!

## Pattern 1e - Overlapping diamonds

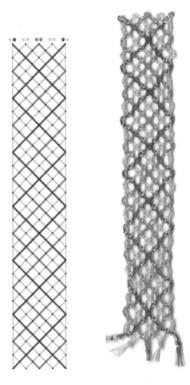

Now we have four coloured pairs, two purple and two red. If started where shown, you get this effect of overlapping diamonds.

We are still working this lace exactly the same as the previous patterns.

There are several more pieces that you could work with two colours (or even three?) I mentioned for the last pattern how easy it is to design these patterns. Start with a basic pattern, and draw in the lines, this time, of course, using two colours. There is a double zigzag overlap, for example, but I will leave that as an exercise for the reader!

If you don't feel confident enough to design a new pattern, you could just try putting random coloured pairs on starting pins, and see what happens. You will get some boring patterns, I expect, but you may stumble across an interesting one.

# Pattern 1f - Small diamonds

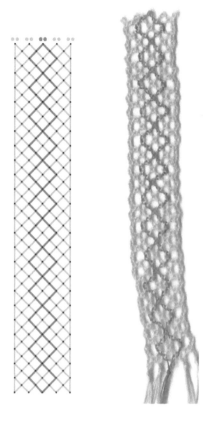

This pattern is different from the previous ones. There are two coloured pairs starting at the centre, rather like pattern 1c. But they are small diamonds. The line changes direction within the lace, as opposed to at the edge.

To do this, you need to use a double Torchon stitch:

You can see from the diagram that the pairs come into the pin from one side, go round the pin, and leave on the same side.

So most of the stitches are Torchon ground (where the coloured pair come in from one side and leave on the other). But where the line on the pattern changes direction, that must be a double Torchon stitch.

This means that it is not as easy to work. You need to follow the coloured line on the pattern, and remember to do a double Torchon ground stitch where required. However, it does give a lot more freedom in the patterns that you can design.

## Pattern 1g - Varying diamonds

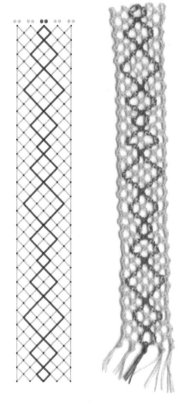

This pattern is similar to pattern 1f, except that the diamonds vary in size. They are worked the same way, except you have to keep an eye on exactly where the coloured pairs change direction. That means you have to work a double Torchon ground stitch (see pattern 1f).

See pattern 1p which uses this pattern to make a collar.

**Tip:** Double Torchon ground stitches need careful tightening. Ordinary Torchon ground can be tightened easily by tugging threads through several stitches, but double Torchon ground makes the threads change direction, and that can lead to looseness or even small loops round the stitch. Pull the threads tight.

# Pattern 1h - Overlapping varying diamonds

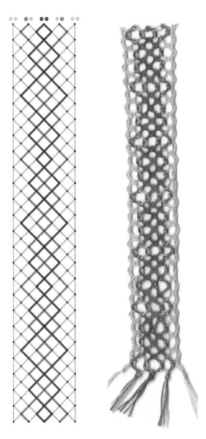

This pattern also has different sized diamonds, but in two colours, red and purple, overlapping each other. That means that the smallest diamond of one colour fits inside the biggest diamond of the other colour.

Since every change of direction is a double Torchon stitch (see pattern 1f), you have to look at the pattern carefully to remember to change direction correctly for each colour. I found it easier if I worked the pattern symmetrically, so every half row that I did on the left was then repeated on the right, but sloping the opposite way.

See pattern 1q for a bigger, but simpler, version of this pattern.

# Pattern 1i - Hearts

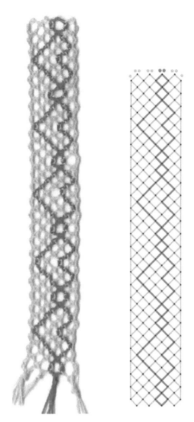

It is possible to make other shapes than diamonds or zigzags. Here are some hearts. They are separated by small diamonds, to make the shape more prominent.

Here are the hearts the right way up:

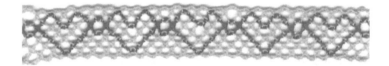

See pattern 1r for a more complicated version of this pattern.

# Pattern 1j - Framed rose 1

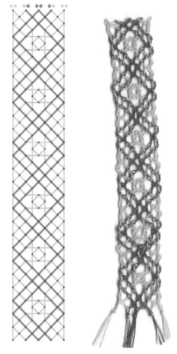

Now we move onto a slightly more complicated set of patterns. There are still only 10 pairs of bobbins. The coloured threads are still restricted to Torchon ground. But now they frame a single unit of rose ground.

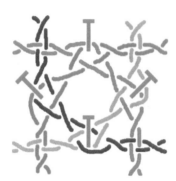

There are four purple pairs. These purple threads travel in a straight line, only changing direction at the edge of the lace, so there are no double Torchon ground stitches.

## Pattern 1k - Framed rose 2

This is the same pattern as the previous one, with two red and two purple pairs. The photo is enlarged so you can see the detail.

This version of this pattern has the coloured pairs travelling in couples from one side to the lace to the other.

One reason for using colour is that you can see exactly how the threads travel through the lace. Lacemakers get a feel for this when making the lace, but anyone looking at lace doesn't understand it. If you use coloured threads, it becomes obvious.

# Pattern 1I - Framed rose 3

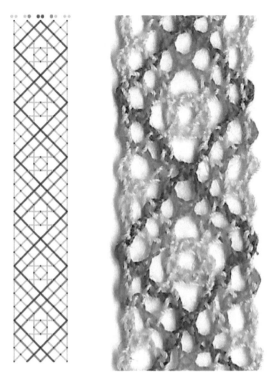

This is still the same pattern, but by starting the red and purple in different places, we get overlapping diamonds.

Each unit of rose ground is framed with one colour on top and a different colour underneath.

You don't have to use these colours. These colours show up well, so the patterns are easy to compare, but you may wish to do something different. You could use white as a background colour, or black. You could make the two colours similar, perhaps two shades of the same colour. How about using gold and silver metallic thread?

At the end of this book, there is a discussion about colour.

## Pattern 1m - Framed rose 4

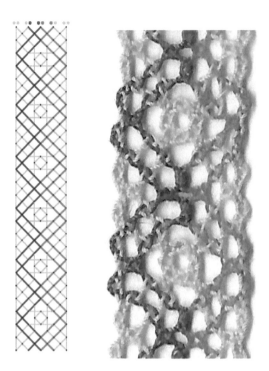

Now we start to use some double Torchon ground stitches (see pattern 1f).

The red and purple pairs travel through the lace like pattern 1k until they reach the centre. Then they are worked in a double Torchon ground stitch, which makes them bounce off each other and change direction. This makes half the lace red and the other half purple.

Remember to keep an eye on the coloured pairs, and the coloured lines in the pattern, to make sure they match.

# Pattern 1n - Framed rose 5

This carries on the idea of using double Torchon ground stitches to change the direction of the coloured pairs. Pattern 1l frames each rose with one colour at the top and another at the bottom, which produces a pattern of overlapping diamonds. But I wanted to frame the rose in a single colour, while still using two colours in the pattern. Since we can change direction, this is possible.

The purple threads stays entirely in the centre, with red nearer the edge. So every rose has an inner frame of purple and an outer frame of red.

There are double Torchon ground stitches in the middle, to bounce back the outer colour. There are also double Torchon ground stitches near the edge, to keep the outer colour outside the inner colour. So this pattern needs a bit of care to cope with all these changes of direction.

# **Pattern 1o -** Framed rose 6

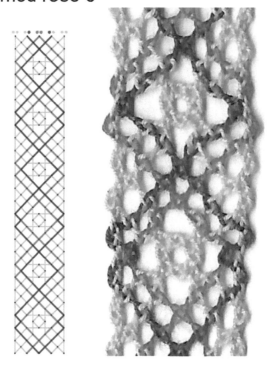

This is similar to the last pattern, but here the roses are framed first purple inside red, then red inside purple.

In fact, it is easier to work than the last pattern. The only double Torchon ground stitches are at the edge. The pairs cross over in the centre, with ordinary Torchon ground stitches.

All these framed roses patterns are identical in pattern. Yet they produce strikingly different effects. All you need to do is start colours in different places, and perhaps put some double Torchon ground stitches to change direction. This shows how powerful colour can be.

## Pattern 1p - varying diamonds collar

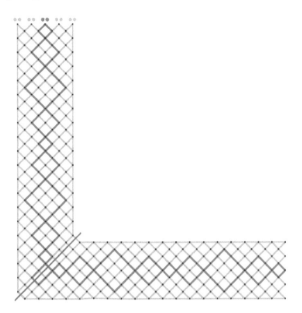

So far, the patterns have been simple, and used only a few bobbins. To end this section, here are a few more complicated patterns.

This is the same pattern as pattern 1g (varying diamonds) but adapted to trim an item of clothing, at the neck. Originally I meant to trim the sleeve edge, but then I noticed that the neck had a square opening at the front. Here is the result:

To make it, you work the first side down to the corner line (which is not part of the pattern). Then you turn the pillow and rearrange the pairs so they hang downwards. Every pair leads naturally on to the next pin, except the two pairs right at the point of the corner. Work these two pairs in an extra cloth stitch and twist (or two), until they reach the next pin. Now carry on working the second half.

The photo demonstrates another point about using colour in lace. Previously the lace has been on a white background, so every colour is visible. But we can be cleverer than that. Before sewing the lace onto my garment, I photographed it against two backgrounds, each being the same as one of the lace colours.

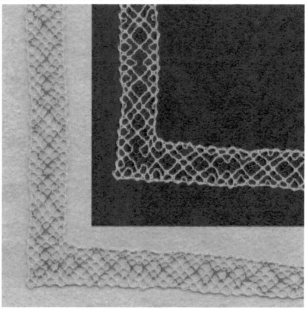

This makes either the pattern, or the background, stand out. My original intention was that the diamonds would show up against my garment. (I am not sure whether I succeeded!) But this demonstrates that you must not only think how the different lace colours work together, but also how they work against any background. It is possible to "lose" a colour in this way.

# Pattern 1q - Bigger overlapping diamonds

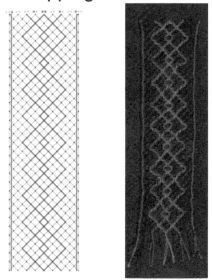

This pattern uses 20 pairs of bobbins, with 14 pairs black, 4 pairs sparkly red and 2 pairs sparkly green.

I liked the idea of pattern 1h (overlapping varying diamonds) but since I was fitting the pattern into a narrow strip, it looks cramped. So this pattern simplifies the diamonds and spreads them out more.

This pattern also has a conventional footside, which allows a new idea. The footside passive is also sparkly red, which frames the whole lace.

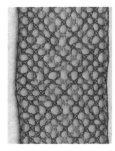

The background colour is black, and the photo above is taken against a dark background to show the different coloured diamonds.

The photo to the left is taken against a pale background.

## Pattern 1r - Double hearts

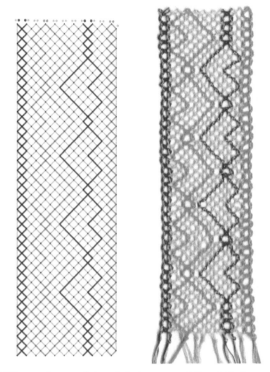

This pattern uses 23 pairs of bobbins, with 15 background colour (pale greenish blue), 4 pairs purple and 4 pairs second orange.

The idea came from pattern 1i (hearts). It uses Winkie pin footside. On each edge, there is a line of little diamonds made using 2 pairs of coloured threads, using double Torchon ground stitches to connect it to the rest of the lace.

The hearts are bigger than pattern 1i. There are two lines of hearts, which fit together. These are different colours.

You may find my choice of colours rather lurid! They are psychedelic colours (from the 1960s), and the hearts represent "All you need is Love". Of course, you can choose your own colours.

## Pattern 1s - Roses inside hearts

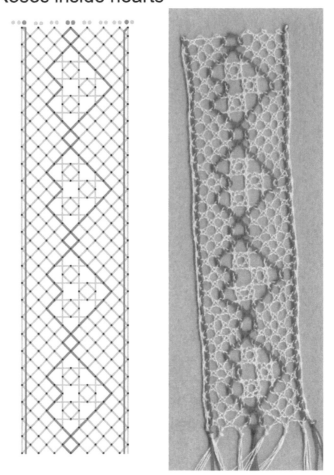

This pattern uses 17 pairs of bobbins (13 background and 4 red pairs).

This is similar to pattern 1i, but with rose ground inside rather than Torchon ground. There is a twisted footside, with red passive pairs. If you prefer, you could make the passives a different colour, or leave them as the background colour.

Here is the pattern the other way up:

## Pattern 1t - Rainbow mat

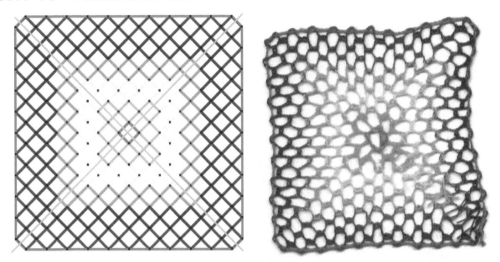

To finish this section, here is a colourful mat using the colours of the rainbow. It uses 12 pairs of bobbins, 2 pairs of each colour.

Like all square mats, it is worked a quarter at a time. The grey corner lines are not part of the pattern – they show where you start and end each quarter. When you have finished one quarter, turn the pillow, and rearrange all the bobbins so they hang down properly in the new direction. Then continue working.

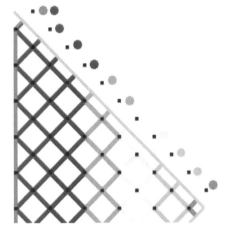

The edge is Winkie pin footside, and all stitches are double Torchon ground, This makes it easy to work (once you have hung the bobbins in the right order – see left), but the colours and making it into a mat produces a striking effect.

# Torchon ground – Summary

- Torchon ground: a pair of bobbins stays together, and travels diagonally through the lace. This can be high-lighted by making this pair a different colour to the rest.
- Winkie pin footside: a pair travelling diagonally one way makes a sharp turn at the edge, and then travels diagonally the other way.
- Double Torchon ground: a pair travelling diagonally one way makes a sharp turn at a pin, and travels diagonally the other way.
- A conventional footside is not suitable if a coloured pair needs to turn sharply at an edge. However, if the coloured pairs stay away from the edge, it doesn't matter what footside you use.
- The passives of any footside can be coloured. They produce a vertical line at or near the edge, which can frame the central pattern.

Using these stitches, you can design sloping lines, diamonds, zigzags, hearts, etc. If you use two colours, these shapes can overlap or frame or bounce off each other.

Pattern 1a can be used as a blank to design your own narrow patterns. If you want something bigger, go to this page on my website:

**www.theedkins.co.uk/jo/lace/make.htm**

and choose one of the "square grids for strips". I suggest using the "lines" grid. You can print this off, then draw your own pattern on it. Your coloured lines must follow the grey lines, but of course you can change direction at any pin. Draw in the edges as straight lines joining the pins vertically.

# Cloth fan headsides

Headsides can cause problems when you use colour, since some of the pairs in the headside leave it to be used in the rest of the lace. Colouring those pairs spoils the shape of the headside. However, if you are careful, there are ways to colour a headside to make it stand out more from the rest of the lace, not less.

A cloth fan is a simple headside. The lines in the diagrams represent a pair of threads. There are passive pairs going downwards. The worker pair travels across the passives in rows, with a pin at each end of the row. Most passives join and leave the fan, but the edge passive pair stays inside.

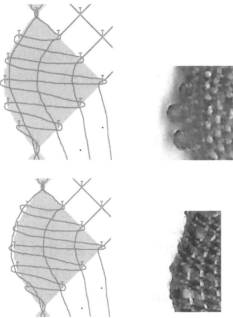

At the edge of the fan, you can pin between the workers and the edge pair, but that tends to produce little loops at the edge. I prefer to pin inside the edge pair, to make a smooth edge. You can use either technique, as you prefer.

Every stitch in a cloth fan is made of cloth stitch. In this diagram, each line represents a thread.

## Pattern 2a - Coloured fans

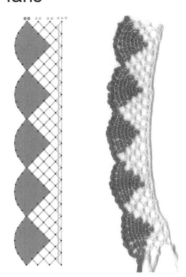

This is a simple pattern, using headside fans, Torchon ground and a twisted footside. It only uses 9 pairs of bobbins. The two pairs on the left are both red (worker and edge pairs). This colours all the fans, and makes them stand out from the ground.

**Tip:** Fans can be tricky. If you over-tighten the passives, you flatten the curve of the edge. While working the fan, tug the passives to the left. As these passives leave the fan, tighten to remove loops, but no more than that. This will preserve the curve of the passives.

Lace with fan headsides tend to bow, as the footside is tight, while the headside is floppy (see photo of lace). Try pulling the headside and footside apart. But the curve may persist. If you sew the footside to something, then the footside will straighten and the fans take up a slightly wavy position, which is quite attractive.

# Pattern 2b - Alternate coloured fans

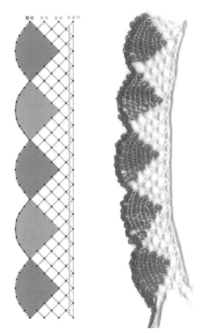

It is obvious from the last pattern that it is the worker pair which colour the fans. So why did we have two pairs coloured? It makes things easier to work, and this version of the same pattern shows why.

Set up the pattern the same, but this time make the two edge pairs different colours. The red pair (on the outside) is the worker pair. Use them to work the first fan until you get to the bottom pin. You will find that the green pair is now on the outside (unless you've missed a pinhole somewhere!) So it is natural to make the green pair the workers, and work them across the others as above. This means that you get alternate coloured fans, as above, which is quite pretty.

It is quite likely that you changed worker pairs from one fan to another in the last pattern, but since they were both the same colour, you didn't notice. So if you want to colour fan headsides, make the edge pair the same colour, and it won't bother you which pair are workers at any point. Workers use more thread than passives, as well, and this helps spread this between two pairs.

## Pattern 2c - Choosing colour of fans

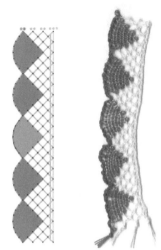

The last pattern shows how the workers in fans tend to alternate, but how do you stop this happening? This pattern shows how you can choose which pair are workers, and so can colour the fans as required.

At the start of each fan, there are two pairs of different colours. Decide what colour you want the fan. That pair will be the workers. Use them to work the first row in whatever direction feels natural to you. It could be that the different fans might be worked in slightly different ways, but it won't be obvious in the final lace.

It is important to realise that the fans are coloured by the colour of the workers, but you will still see the colour of the passives as well. The worker colour does dominate, though. The passives will show more if the pattern is bigger or the thread is thinner. So you can experiment with different pattern sizes and thread thicknesses to see different effects. It is not even necessary to have all threads the same thickness. Thicker worker threads show up better against thinner passives. There is a limit to how thick a thread can be for a specific size of pattern, as the cloth stitch starts to coggle.

## Pattern 2d - Checkerboard fans

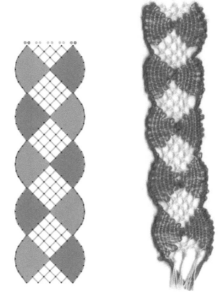

This pattern needs 10 pairs of bobbins, with 2 red pairs, 2 green pairs, and 6 pairs as background.

Each edge is worked similar to the headside of pattern 2b, producing alternate coloured fans. However, the fans meet in the centre of the lace. So you need to work half of the left fan, leaving the workers at the point of the fan, in the middle. Then work half of the right fan in the same way. That means that the two coloured workers are together. Work them as cloth stitch, pin, cloth stitch.

Now they can work the rest of the two fans, in turn.

This pattern has headsides on both sides, and so it avoids the slight bending of lace you get with a footside and headside.

## Pattern 2e - Butterfly fans

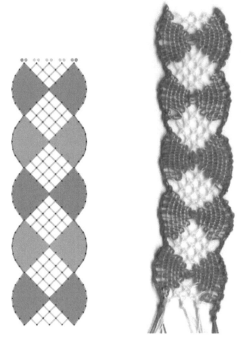

This is the same as pattern 2d, except the colours are the same on both sides. This is caused simply by which pins the coloured pairs start from.

I think the fans look like butterflies!

In these fan patterns, I have used strongly contrasting colours. You may prefer to use colours close together, perhaps mid blue and dark blue, which will produce a more subtle effect.

This pattern and the last have the fans meeting in the middle of the lace, with the two pairs of workers work through each other and back again, round the pin, so they return to their own side of the lace. What would happen if these workers swapped over to the other side of the lace? See next pattern.

# Pattern 2f - Sideways butterfly fans

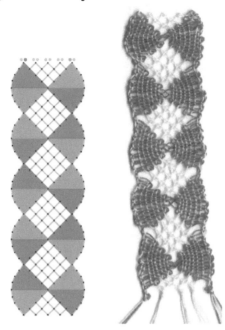

This pattern has ten pairs of bobbins, like the previous patterns, but it only has two coloured pairs, a red pair starting on the left, and a green pair on the right. All passives, even the edge ones, are the background colour.

Work half of each fan until both coloured worker pairs are in the middle of the lace. Work them as half stitch, pin, cross (or perhaps you may prefer to think of it as cloth stitch with a pin in the middle).

This means that the two workers swap over to the other fan. So each half of the fan is coloured differently.

However, where one fan leads onto the fan below, the coloured pair must remain as the workers. See pattern 2c for how to do this.

Can you see the sideways butterflies?

## Pattern 2g - Multi-coloured fans

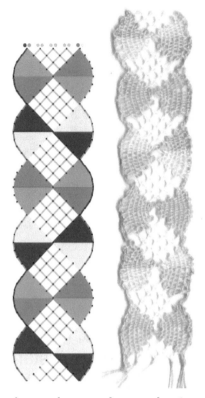

This pattern combines changing colours between one fan and another, and swapping over coloured workers where fans meet.

There are two colours starting on the left, one as workers and one as edge pair, and two different colours similarly on the right. The coloured workers swap over half way through the fan (see pattern 2f). The coloured workers and edge pairs swap over between fans (see pattern 2b).

There are five colours (including background). I have used pale shades, with white as a background. You can choose which colours you like, of course.

You can also vary which you swap workers or not, both half way through the fans, and between fans. You could even do this at random.

## Pattern 2h - Striped fans

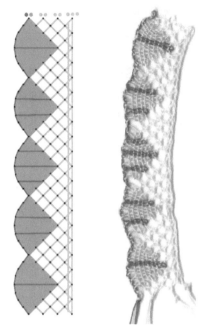

Now for a new technique. This doesn't need a double line of fans like the last few patterns, so I have gone back to the simpler pattern of pattern 2c. This has a dark green edge passive pair, and pale green as workers of the fans.

Normally, the workers of a fan work through the edge passive, round the pin, and back again, so they stay as the workers.

However, we can change the workers if we wish. This will make the dark green edge pair into the workers for the next row, and leave the old workers as edge passives for a bit.

The new workers have to work a double row (there and back again) before returning to the edge, where they can be swapped again, if you choose.

In this pattern, the edge passives become workers just for one double row at a time. The different fans have this row in different places, giving a striped effect. The middle fan changes workers every double row.

## Pattern 2i - Multiple butterflies

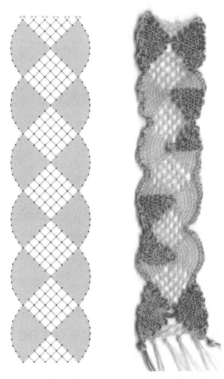

This pattern has half fans. Unlike pattern 2f, the fan's workers from one side cannot travel to the other. Instead, like pattern 2h, the edge passive pair becomes the worker pair half way through the fan.

The background pairs are pale blue, and there are only two dark blue pairs. These colour the top butterfly. The pale blue pairs become workers for the next fans. Half way down the right-hand side of the second fan, the dark blue edge pair swaps with the pale blue worker pair, to become workers in their turn. The dark blue workers continue in the next fan to make the sideways butterfly. And so on.

You may feel that we're spending too much time on such a narrow pattern. It is useful to see what we can do with these two touching headsides, because much of it also works when a fan touches a diamond or zigzag (see next section).

# Pattern 2j - Path of roses

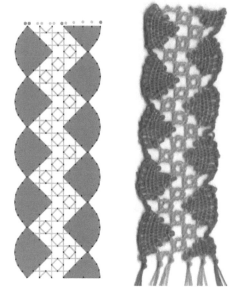

Now for something completely different! This is still a narrow pattern (only 12 pairs of bobbins) and has fans on both sides. But the two lines of fans are offset from each other. In between, there is a line of rose ground.

The colour of the fans are much simpler from most of the previous patterns. Each line of fans has two red pairs, one as workers, and one as edge passives. This means it doesn't matter whether you use the same pair from one fan to the next or not.

This pattern works well if worked in a single colour throughout. But colouring the fans gives a bold effect, and emphasises the rose ground well.

Remember, you can take any pattern with fan headside, and colour it as you please. You can keep it simple, like this, or have fans with different colours or half fans, as in previous patterns. I think this pattern looks best with just red and pink.

# Summary – Cloth fans

- The same worker pair is used throughout cloth stitch. If this pair has a different colour to the rest of the pairs, this will colour the cloth shape, such as a fan headside.

- Most of the passives in a fan enter and leave the fan to rejoin the rest of the lace. But the edge pair of passives stays within the fans. So these can have their own colour. This gives a different coloured edge to the fan.

- The edge passives of one fan can become the workers of the next. This will give alternate coloured fans.

- By choosing whether to swap edge pairs and workers from one fan to another, or not, you can decide which colour the fan is.

- The edge passives and the workers can also be swapped within the fan. The new workers will have to do a minimum of two rows (there and back again) before returning to the edge, where they can be swapped again, if you like. Or the new workers can work more rows, such as half a fan.

- If the edge passives and the workers are the same colour (but different to the rest of the lace) then you don't need to worry which pair to use as workers for the next fan. Use whichever seems natural.

- If the cloth fans touch another cloth shape at the point of the fan (for example, fans on the other side of the lace), then the workers of both shapes can be swapped over at that point. If these workers are different colours, this will colour the first half of the fans differently to the second half, giving half fans.

~~~~~~~~~~

# Half stitch fans

It is trickier to colour fans made of half stitch than of cloth stitch, but it is possible.

Cloth stitch has a pair of workers involved in every stitch. If those workers are coloured, then the whole shape is coloured (although the passives' colour may show through).

Half stitch does not have a pair of workers. Instead, the stitch is worked from one pair from the last stitch and a new pair. The stitch is half stitch, and that means that the pairs get split up. So you do not get the same pair going onto the next stitch.

However, you do get a single thread (or bobbin) which is used in every stitch in a row. If that single thread is coloured, then the whole row is coloured. We can call this thread the worker thread (rather than a pair of workers). If we take a little care to make sure that this same thread is the worker thread for the next row, then we can colour the whole fan.

The passives are different for half stitch as well. Instead of hanging straight down (or bowed slightly outwards for a fan), they divide, with the threads travelling diagonally. That means that we can't have a pair of edge passives. However (again with a little care) we can persuade a single thread to stay at the edge. So rather than a coloured pair of workers and a coloured passive edge pair, we can have a single coloured worker thread, and a single coloured passive thread. But you do need to be careful that these coloured threads stay as worker and edge, and don't become one of the other passives instead! As I said – tricky, but possible.

Another problem is that a single thread doesn't provide as much colour as a pair, so the colouring is more muted.

## Pattern 2k - Half stitch fans

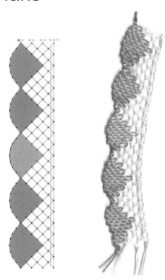

This is similar to pattern 2c, with 9 pairs. There are 8 pairs of background colour, and the left-most pair is red and green threads knotted together. You can see the knot.

For each row of half stitch, before you start, make sure that the edge coloured thread is the left-most thread. Also make sure that the worker thread is the second thread in.

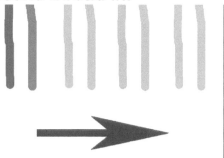

For rows going the other way, the threads should look like this. If you get this wrong, then one of the background threads will become the worker.

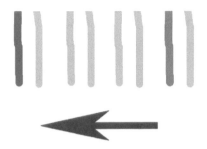

If the coloured threads at the start of a row are in the wrong place (and they will be!), then twist the pairs involved until they are right. I found this to be one pair twisted going one way, and two pairs twisted, one at each end, going the other way.

A little care between fans will even let you swap over the coloured edge thread with the coloured worker thread, so different fans can be different colours, as you choose.

# Pattern 2l - Mixed fans

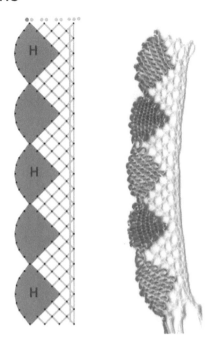

In the previous pattern, the worker thread and the edge thread were different colours. Here, they are the same colour. This means that you can change from half stitch fans to cloth stitch fans, if you choose.

The pattern marks the half stitch fans with H, so you start with a half stitch fan. This is worked as in pattern 2k. At the end of this fan, you need to get both coloured threads together, so they can be used as a pair of workers for the cloth stitch fan. At the end of the cloth fan, the coloured pair must be on the far left, so they can start the middle half stitch fan.

It may be necessary to do one more, or less, stitch, to get the coloured pair in the correct place between fans.

Using colour for the worker pair (cloth stitch) or worker thread (half stitch) high-lights the pattern of the threads in these two different stitches.

You should feel quite proud of yourself if you can get this to work!

## Pattern 2m - Half stitch half fans

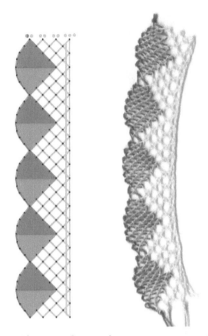

If you have a red worker thread and a green edge thread, as in pattern 2k, then you can have half fans of the different colours.

Remember to knot the two different coloured threads together to make a pair. The left thread will be the edge thread, and the other the worker thread. Work the top half of the fan, making sure that the edge thread stays at the edge, and the worker thread (second in) is the correct colour – see pattern 2k. Twist the end pairs if the colours are in the wrong place.

Half way through the fan, when the worker thread is next to the edge thread, change the edge and worker pair over, by twisting if necessary, and continue with the rest of the fan.

If you want, you could keep the worker thread the same into the top half of the next fan, like pattern 2f. But I have switched them back again, to make every fan the same.

# Pattern 2n - Half stitch butterflies

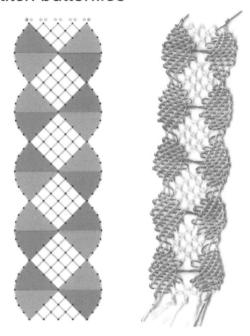

This is the half stitch version of pattern 2f. There is a red worker thread on the left and a green worker thread on the right. The edge threads have to be the background colour. This means that the coloured worker thread and the background thread have to be knotted together to make the pair on each side.

Work half the fan. There should be two pairs in the centre, each with a coloured thread and a background thread. Work these in a half stitch, resting on a pin. That takes them to the opposite side's fan, where they work the second half of the fans.

I haven't given all possible patterns involving half stitch fans. But I hope you can work out how to adapt the cloth fan patterns to half stitch. Remember, coloured pairs in cloth stitch become coloured single threads in half stitch.

# Summary – Half stitch fans

- Unlike cloth stitch, the pairs in half stitch get split up. However, one thread is used for every stitch in a row, and if twisted appropriately, for the whole shape. If this thread is a different colour to the rest, this will colour the cloth shape, such as a fan.
- There is not a pair which stays at the edge, but with appropriate twisting, you can keep a single thread at the edge.
- The edge thread of one fan can become the worker thread of the next. This will give alternate coloured fans.
- By choosing the edge thread and worker thread from one fan to another, or not, you can decide the colour of the fan.
- The edge and worker threads can also be swapped within the fan. The new worker thread will have to do a minimum of two rows (there and back again) before returning to the edge, where they can be swapped again, if you like. Or it can work more rows, to colour half a fan.
- If the half stitch fans touch another half stitch shape at the point of the fan (for example, fans on the other side of the lace), then the worker threads of both shapes can be swapped over at that point. If these workers are different colours, this will colour the first half of the fans differently to the second half, giving half fans.
- If the edge and worker threads of a half stitch fan are the same colour, then at the end of the fan they can be brought together as worker pair for a cloth fan. This cloth fan will have the passive edge pair as background colour.

# Fans and ground

The previous patterns have either coloured fans or ground, but of course you can do both. There is one style of lace which specialises in this. Lace from Panama is called *mundillo* and it is used to make their national dress, called *pollera*. This uses coloured workers in cloth fans. Since this is cloth stitch, we are using coloured pairs, not threads. The ground is usually simple Torchon ground, and the footside is Winkie pin, with two passives.

Pattern 2b shows how you can have alternate coloured fans, but these Panama patterns are cleverer than that. The fans do not touch other. Instead, they are one or more pinholes apart. So a fan may have one colour as workers, and a second colour at the edge. At the end of the fan, the workers in the first colour become the edge pair for the next fan. The second colour leaves the headside altogether, and crosses the ground to reach the footside. Meanwhile a third coloured pair crosses the ground in the opposite direction, from footside to headside to become the new workers.

That sounds very complicated. But look at the next few patterns, and you will see that the pattern is very logical, and natural to work. Start where you're supposed to, and make sure that the coloured threads are in the right place, doing the right stitch, and it will work!

## Pattern 2o - Three colour fans

This is a very small Panama pattern. There are only 7 pairs, with red, blue and green pairs and the rest white (including 2 passive pairs in the Winkie pin footside). This makes a narrow piece of lace, which is apt to twist. This doesn't matter if you sew it to something.

While working the cloth stitch fan, there is one colour as worker pair, a second colour as edge pair, and a third colour isn't in the fan at all, but is part of the Torchon ground. At the end of the fan, the worker pair travels to the next pinhole to become the edge pair for the next fan. (If you want, you can give this pair an extra twist to strengthen the part between the two fans.) The old edge pair leaves the fan to travel to the footside, crossing over the third coloured pair, which is about to join the new fan as the worker pair.

# **Pattern 2p -** Four colour fan

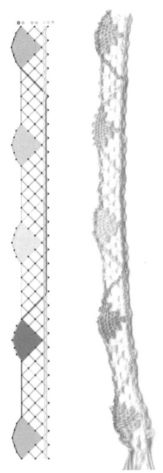

This Panama pattern is similar to pattern 2o, with only 7 pairs in all, but with 4 different coloured pairs. The fans are even further apart. The edge pair of a fan leaves the fan at its end and travels across the ground, like the last pattern. However this doesn't bounce off the footside.

The footside is a little odd. The passives are two of the coloured pairs. When a coloured edge pair leaves a fan, it travels across the ground to join the footside. The coloured pair that it replaces travels back across the ground to join the next fan.

The swapping of workers leads to each fan being a different colour, and the colours travelling through the ground make their own pattern. Perhaps it makes the footside a little over-colourful! This could be hidden if you were sewing the lace onto fabric.

## Pattern 2q - Wide four colour fans

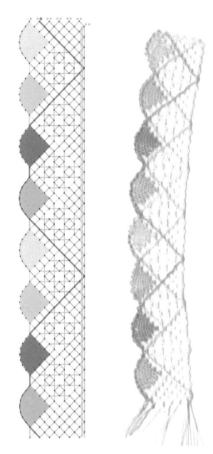

This Panama pattern has four colours, but is more like pattern 2o than pattern 2p. It is a wider piece of lace (14 pairs). The footside passives are not coloured. The coloured pairs bounce off the footside and return to colour the next fan. These coloured pairs crossing the lace frame an area, filled with rose stitch.

This is a simplified version of a Panama pattern. They tend to like doing different grounds in their framed areas, but I wanted to keep this simple, and concentrate on the colours. The rose stitch doesn't show up in the photo, as it is white threads on a white background. I wanted to emphasise the coloured threads rather than the grounds. It would show better against a coloured fabric, or you could change the ground colour.

# Pattern 2r - Coloured fan passive

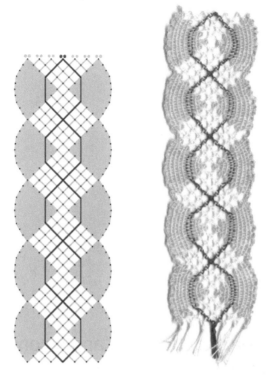

So far, we have had coloured workers, and coloured edge passives, and coloured ground. What happens if we colour one of the other passive pairs of the fan? It needs a little thought, because the pair will leave the fan to enter the ground. However, this can make a pleasing pattern, as above.

There are 14 pairs, with 8 background. Each fan has 2 pale blue pairs, worker and edge. In the middle, there are 2 dark blue pairs. These get worked the same as the background pairs.

This pattern shows how the colour of passive pairs gets muted as they pass through the fan. So this pattern needs a strong contrast between the fan worker colour and the coloured passive. It highlights the difference between cloth stitch and Torchon ground, showing how a pair of threads travel through the lace. You can learn a lot about lace through using colour!

## Pattern 2s - Separate fan and ground

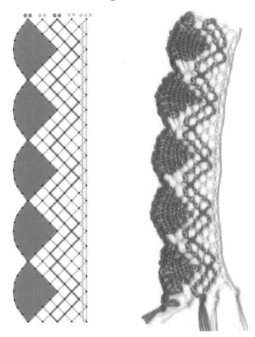

This pattern uses 11 pairs of bobbins, and a conventional twisted passive footside. It shows how colouring fans and ground can be separate patterns but make a unified design. The colouring of the fans is like pattern 2a, and the design in the ground uses a mixture of Torchon ground, and double Torchon ground where the line changes direction, as in pattern 1f.

The coloured pairs in the fans and the ground never meet, and if you wanted, you could make them different colours. You could also make the edge pair a different colour, and have alternate coloured fans, or half fans, or (with a different colour combination) half stitch fans. Once you understand the different tricks you can play with colour and fans, described in this section, you can have fun altering a simple fan headside pattern in any way you choose.

# Shapes within lace

Torchon lace has many shapes, worked in cloth stitch or half stitch, in the body of the lace. The most common are diamonds and zigzags, but there are also hearts and triangles.

Cloth stitch shapes have a single pair of workers, and half stitch shapes can have a single worker thread, just as fan headsides do. This means there is the potential to colour them, but there are a couple of problems.

You expect a headside to have the fans touching each other (although the Panama patterns do separate the fans). However, diamonds do not necessarily touch each other in the same way. If they don't, then you need to work out some way to get the worker pair from one diamond to the next, possibly going through ground.

There is also a problem if you try to use two colours on the same shape. With fans, you can "hide" a pair by making it the edge pair, where the eye tends to ignore it. Diamonds do not have an edge pair.

However, let's start with a simple pattern which doesn't have these problems.

## Pattern 3a - Cloth diamonds

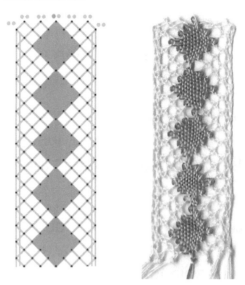

This pattern uses 14 pairs, with only one pair coloured. It has a twisted footside, Torchon ground and cloth diamonds. The diamonds touch.

This means that the same pair of workers can be used for all diamonds. If this pair uses coloured thread, then all diamonds will be coloured the same way. This makes the diamonds stand out from the ground even more than they would usually.

# Pattern 3b - Half stitch diamonds

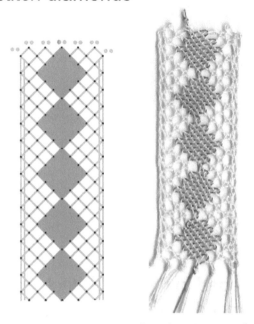

This is exactly the same pattern as the last one (pattern 3a) but the diamonds are worked in half stitch. One thread is coloured rather than a pair. This means that a pair has to have a coloured thread and a background thread knotted together.

Half stitch doesn't have a worker pair, as the pairs change from one stitch to the next. However, it does use the same thread for one row of half stitch. If you twist the end pair before starting the next row, then this thread will be used in every stitch in the next row as well. So if this is coloured, you colour the diamond.

To make sure this happens, make sure that the second thread at the start of each row is the coloured thread. This becomes the worker thread.

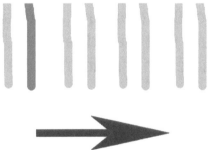

# Pattern 3c - Mixed diamonds

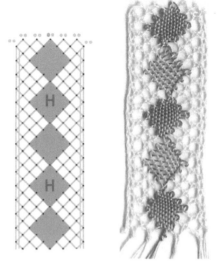

In pattern 2l, we managed to mix cloth stitch and half stitch fans. Is this possible with diamonds? Yes, but it's a bit tricky. Cloth stitch requires a coloured pair, but half stitch only has a coloured thread. With fans, we could "hide" the spare coloured thread at the edge. Half stitch diamonds also have a edge, but it's not the same. In the top half of the diamond, pairs are joining the diamond, and you must make sure that the edge thread stays at the edge, and isn't shunted into the main part of the fan. The worker thread (red) and the edge thread (green) must be like this:

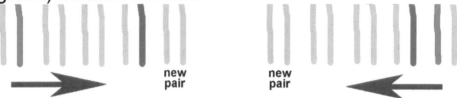

new
pair

new
pair

But in the bottom part of the diamond, pairs are being discarded, and you must make sure that the edge thread doesn't get discarded as well! The worker and edge thread must be like this:

Oddly enough, for most rows, all that's needed is to twist the pair with the worker thread. But you need to position the threads correctly at the top, and between the top half and bottom half. You also need to get the two coloured threads together at the bottom for the next cloth diamond.

## Pattern 3d - Two colour diamonds

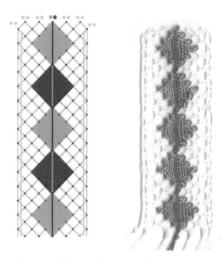

Back to cloth stitch. Pattern 2b shows how we can have fans of two colours, by having one coloured pair as workers and leave the other coloured pair at the edge, then swapping them for the next fan. Can we do this with diamonds?

Yes and no. We can't leave a coloured pair at the edge, because the passives in diamonds don't work like that. What we can do is have the central passive pair as a different colour. If you look closely at the picture, you can see that there is a darker coloured passive pair going through the middle of the diamond. This can then be swapped with the coloured worker pair for the next diamond.

Unfortunately this central passive pair is fairly visible. I have used fairly dark green and blue, which are similar colours, so the difference is not too bad. It can show up a lot more - see pattern 3f.

## Pattern 3e - Two lines of diamonds

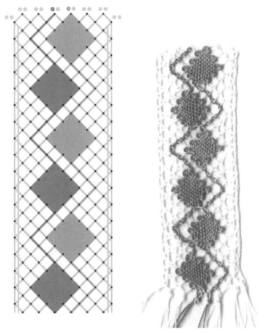

You can have two colours of diamonds without a diamond having to share both colours. The green pair colours one diamond, then leaves the diamond to travel across the ground to get to another diamond further down. Meanwhile the red pair colours a different diamond, and also travels across the ground to get to yet another diamonds. In this pattern, the diamonds overlap to make a staggered effect.

This patter uses 16 pairs, including a green pair and a red pair. Remember to use a double Torchon ground stitch to make the coloured pair change direction while going through the ground (see pattern 1f).

## Pattern 3f Four colour diamonds

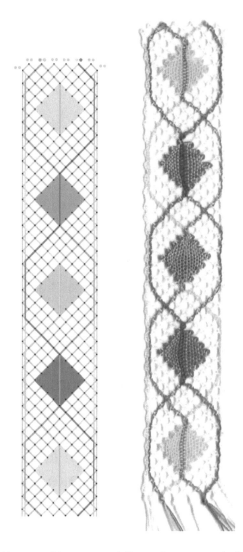

This is a Panama pattern. It uses 16 pairs, and 4 coloured pairs. These are used to colour the diamonds, or go through the centre of the diamonds, or travel through the ground, or swap with one of the passives in the footside. See pattern 3d for another example of a coloured pair as central passives in a diamond, and pattern 2p for the use of footsides.

In pattern 3d, the two colours in the diamonds were close to each other in an attempt to hide the central passives. Here they are deliberately different, yellow/blue and red/green. So rather than the passives getting hidden, they become part of the pattern.

## Pattern 3g - Chequerboard diamonds

This striking pattern is bigger than previous ones. It uses 19 pairs, including 3 red pairs and 3 yellow pairs.

The two lines of diamonds in the middle are exactly like the diamonds in pattern 3a. At the edge, there are triangles of cloth stitch. These are similar to fans, but without the curved edge. Outside these (unlike fans!), there is a Winkie pin footside with a single twisted passive. In alternate rows, the worker pair from the triangle travels just to the edge of the triangle, or crosses the footside passive to go round the pin and back again. Both triangle worker pair, and the footside passive pair are coloured, which gives a good strong coloured edge to the lace.

There is no ground at all!

## Pattern 3h - Zigzags

Now we move onto zigzags. This is still a bigger pattern, including 2 green pairs, workers for the zigzags.

These are very thin zigzags. Instead of having regular bends, these are erratic, which makes a more interesting pattern. Zigzags take in pairs from one side and discard them from the other, changing which side is which at the bends. This pattern needs a little care, particularly for the short sides.

The zigzag is coloured by its workers, similar to the other cloth shapes. They surround single units of rose ground. The zigzags don't touch. They are independent of each other, lying side by side.

I have made a mistake in working this – see the photo above. Spot it? I have left out one of the rose ground cross-overs in the top rose.

# Pattern 3i - Snake

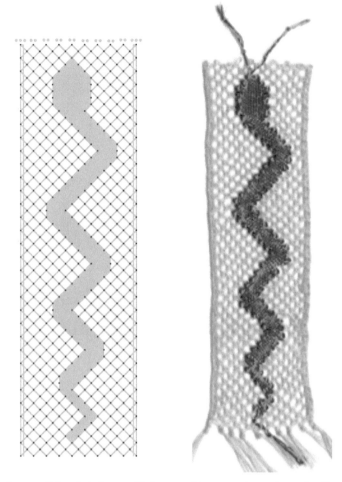

This uses 22 pairs of bobbins. It is quite a simple cloth zigzag pattern, with Torchon ground and twisted footside. Some of the bends of the zigzag have been smoothed out with straight edges. These have one (or more) pinholes where no pair leaves or joins the ground.

How does the coloured pair join and leave the snake? At the start, there are two pairs with one coloured thread and one background thread. These travel to meet the top of the snake. They are supposed to make the flickering forked tongue! I have deliberately started these two mixed pairs well before the start of the lace to emphasise this. You will need to make sure that the two coloured threads end up next to each other so they can become the workers of the whole snake.

At the bottom, the coloured pair continue on to make the snake's tail.

# Pattern 3j - Cloth and half stitch zigzags

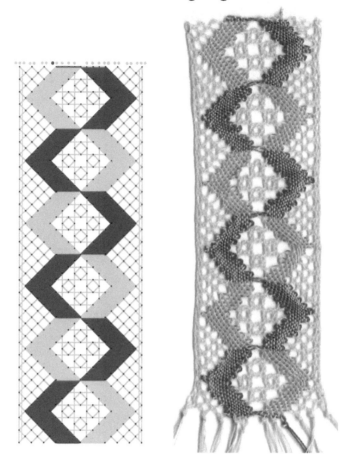

Zigzags can be a mixture of cloth stitch and half stitch. Can we do this with colour? There is a problem because cloth stitch is coloured with a worker pair, but half stitch is coloured with a single thread. In pattern 3c we managed it but it was a bit tricky. However, if the shapes touch, there is another way.

This pattern uses 24 pairs. There are two zigzags, one cloth stitch with dark blue workers and one half stitch with a single mid blue thread. These zigzags touch in the middle of the lace. Work down to that point, so the coloured pair and the pair with the single coloured thread lie next to each other.  Then work a cloth stitch with those two pairs, which will swap them over. This means that the dark blue pair can now work in cloth stitch on the other side, and likewise the mid blue thread in half stitch. See pattern 3b for working in coloured half stitch.

The middle of the zigzags are rose ground, and the rest is Torchon ground and twisted footside, as usual.

# Pattern 3k - Two hearts

This could be used for a card, for a wedding or Valentine, perhaps. It uses 22 pairs, and three colours, red, yellow and blue.

The big shapes are hearts, which are coloured like any other shape. They need the red pair introduced via ground, similar to pattern 1f. The blue diamonds are also linked via ground, similar to pattern 3e. As usual, if the ground pair do a bend, then it is a double Torchon ground stitch. The fans have yellow workers, and blue edge pair, and swap them between fans, like pattern 2b.

The colours are a little bright! Choose which colours you want, perhaps shades of pink rather than yellow and blue. This is the lace the correct way up.

# Summary – Shapes within the lace

- In cloth shapes, the worker pair, if coloured, will colour the shape. For half stitch, a coloured worker thread will colour the shape.
- If the shapes touch vertically (down the lace), then the same worker (pair or thread) can be used, colouring the shapes the same.
- If the shapes do not touch, then the worker pair/thread can travel through the ground to rejoin the next shape. This will be obvious, but acceptable if it makes an attractive pattern within the ground.
- If shapes touch horizontally (across the lace) then you can swap worker pair/thread at that point, to transfer colour or type of stitch. You can do this with touching fans and shapes as well.
- Unlike a fan, in cloth stitch shapes, there is usually no edge pair. However, the central passive pair may stay within the shape (such as in a diamond) and be treated the same way. It will be more visible than the edge of a fan, though. In zigzags, there probably will not be any passive pair that stays within the shape.
- In a half stitch shape, you might be able to persuade a coloured thread (not pair) to remain at the edge, with careful twisting, etc. It is a bit tricky! If managed, it means that you can combine cloth and half stitch shapes with the same pair of workers (and so colour).
- Triangles are a shape which works more like fans than other shapes such as diamonds. Triangles do have an edge pair rather than a central pair.

# Scallop headsides

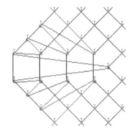

There is a common headside in Torchon lace made of cloth stitch and twist. I call it scallop headside because it looks like a line of shells.

This headside has a single pair of workers throughout. The actual pattern of threads is different to cloth fan headsides, but as far as using colour is concerned, this doesn't matter. Make the worker pair coloured, and you will colour the scallop.

The edge pair stay at the edge, again like cloth fans. That means that you can use all the tricks of colour that we have already used with cloth fans. You can make the edge pair and worker pair different colours, and swap them over between scallops to get alternate colours. You can choose which of the previous edge or worker pair becomes the new worker pair. You can even have half a scallop one colour and half the other, or swap workers at the point if a shape touches it there. I am not going through every possibility! Just go through section 2 and replace the cloth fans with scallops.

Scallops and cloth fans look different. A scallop is more open because the stitches are all cloth stitch and twist. It is harder to tighten as well, since the twists in the stitches tend to trap loops if you aren't careful.

## Pattern 4a - Scallops

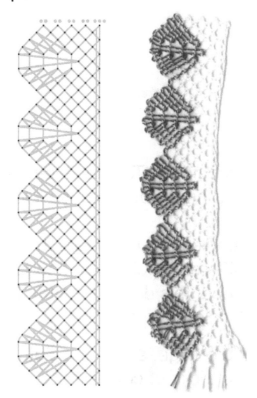

Here is a very simple pattern using 11 pairs of bobbins, with one blue pair as workers of the scallops.

The edge pair are in the background colour, so the only colour is the workers. This shows the basic pattern of the scallops very clearly.

As the same workers are used in every scallop, it is important to make the right stitch at the pin at the end of one scallop (which is also the first pin of the next). To keep the workers the same, the stitch should be cloth stitch and twist, pin, cloth stitch and twist. To swap the workers and edge pair, the stitch is half stitch, pin, half stitch. Here, we keep the workers the same.

# Pattern 4b - Pilgrimage

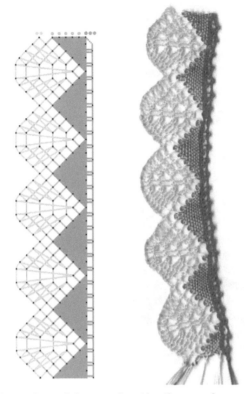

This pattern uses 10 pairs. Here, both the edge and worker pairs are coloured pale brown. This gives a rounded edge rather than a spiky one, as in the previous pattern. Then there are three green pairs, providing the edge pair and worker pair of the triangle, and the passive of the Winkie pin twisted footside. The background colour is white, which doesn't really show up in the photo!

This is a simpler version of some lace I made for a friend who travelled on the pilgrim trail to Santiago in Spain. The trail is through mountains, and the symbol of the pilgrim is a scallop. Hence the name of this pattern.

## Pattern 4c - Flowers

This pattern has 16 pairs. There are a dark pink pair and a pale pink pair for the fans and scallops (the flowers), and 2 green pairs for the zigzags (leaves).

The zigzags are a little tricky to work, as they vary in length and width. Make sure you find all the pinholes, particularly on the inside of the bends. There is also a stitch or two of Torchon ground between the flowers as well as next to the footside. I must admit that while working it, I forgot to keep to cloth stitch for the fans and cloth stitch and twist for the scallops, and had to undo a bit!

The last flower is the same as the first, so you could repeat the pattern. There are other possible patterns (and colours). For example: red scallop, pink fan, red scallop, pink fan. Or red scallop, pink scallop, red fan, pink fan. Or red scallop, red fan, red scallop, pink scallop, pink fan, pink scallop. Or you could just change colours and fan/scallops at random! Remember that the non-used colour is kept at the edge.

## Pattern 4d - Mixing colours

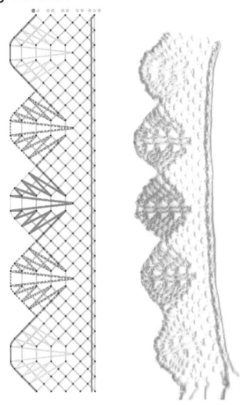

So far, apart from half stitch, all the coloured pairs have been the same colour. What happens if a pair has two threads of different colours? This pattern explores this. It is the same as pattern 4a, except there is dark pink at the edge, and pale pink as workers, which colours the first scallop.

Before the second scallop, these two pairs do a half stitch, pin. This makes both edge and worker pairs have one pale pink thread and one dark pink thread. This gives the second fan – darker than the first.

Between the second and the third scallops, another half stitch gets the pairs with both threads the same colour again. So the third scallop is now dark pink. The fourth is like the second, and the fifth back to pale pink. The footside passive are dark pink – remember, you can always colour footside passives.

It isn't just scallops (and fans) that can do this. Any coloured pair anywhere can have threads different colours. The result will be a mottled combination of the two colours.

# Summary – Scallop headsides

Scallop headsides have a worker pair and an edge pair exactly like cloth fans (although they are worked in a different stitch, cloth stitch and twist, and the workers travel a different path). This means that every colour effect with fans can also be done with scallops. The final effect will look different, as scallops are more open headside than fans.

In particular, scallops can be coloured with workers. The edge pair can be coloured the same as the workers, or a different colour, or background colour. The workers and edge pair, if different colours, can be swapped over between scallops, to alternate colour.

Scallops and fans can be mixed within one headside.

Not only can you have different colours for edge and worker pairs, you can have different colours between the threads of a single pair. This will produce a mottled coloured effect somewhere between the two colours. This will work anywhere you have a coloured pair. It doesn't work for half stitch, which only has a single worker thread.

# Rose ground

We have used rose ground already, such as in Pattern 1j. But there it was in the background colour, with other parts of the lace coloured to make a frame for it. Now we are going to investigate how we can colour rose ground itself.

The other grounds that we have investigated, Torchon ground and double Torchon ground, are simple. Every stitch is the same, made with two pairs, and has the same behaviour. A unit of rose ground needs four pairs, and by colouring those pairs in different ways, you get different effects.

I am going to give some minimal patterns. These are diamonds of rose ground, with just a line of Torchon ground round to give an edge. This type of pattern is a good way to see exactly what is happening. Then there are other patterns which use these effects in a more controlled way.

I suggest that you are confident in working rose ground before trying these patterns. Having different coloured pairs coming into and leaving a rose ground unit can confuse you quite easily!

# Pattern 5a - Alternating couples of pairs

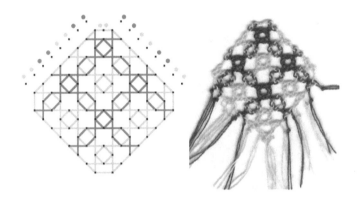

This minimal pattern uses 18 pairs. The rose ground uses 8 pairs of dark blue and 8 pale blue. The remaining 2 pairs are pale blue. They provide the line of Torchon ground round the edge. You could choose different colours.

This pattern starts on the slant, so there are false starting pin holes. At the start, put pins in these holes, and hang the bobbins from them. Do the two slanting rows of Torchon ground. Then remove all the false pins, and gently pull the threads through. This means that you don't have to reuse the real starting pin as part of the first stitch.

The coloured pairs used in the rose ground start in couples. So the top unit of rose ground is entirely dark blue. The unit below that is pale blue. Units between are mixed. The effect is similar to a tartan.

## Pattern 5b - Five gold rings

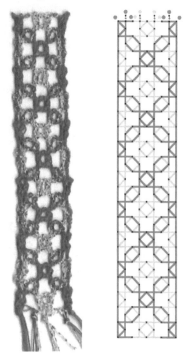

This is a thin strip of rose ground with a Winkie pin footside – only 10 pairs of bobbins. Like pattern 5a, the colours go in couples of pairs – this time gold and red. At the edge of the strip, sometimes there is half a unit of rose ground. This is not too hard to work. Every pin is half stitch, pin, half stitch. The cross-overs are cloth stitch and twist. The edge is cloth stitch and twist, pin, cloth stitch and twist.

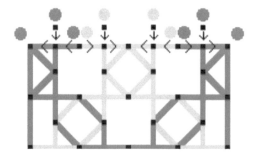

The beginning is a little tricky, as we are starting in the middle of a unit of rose ground. The enlarged picture, above, shows the directions of the threads. There are some false starting pin holes.

I see this as five gold rings, as in The Twelve Days of Christmas.

## Pattern 5c - Alternating pairs

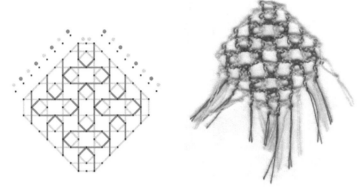

This is the same pattern as pattern 5a, except that the pairs start alternately different colours, instead of starting in couples of pairs. As you see, it produces an entirely different pattern. It is important not to make a mistake. Even leaving out a cross-over messes up the pattern!

If you want, you can finish off by tying reef (square) knots and trimming the ends close. That would be neater. I have left a fringe so you can see how the coloured threads finish.

This type of pattern can be adapted to try out different arrangements of colours, other than the two I've tried. See what happens! You can also try other grounds.   This pattern starts on a diagonal, has no vertical edges, and ends on a diagonal, which makes it easier to figure out how to work it. It also has a wide area of the ground so you can see what is happening.

## Pattern 5d - Alternating pairs edge

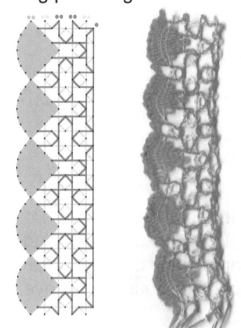

This is using the same design as pattern 5c. It has 11 pairs and 3 colours. The fan has 2 orange pairs. The rose ground has 4 yellow pairs and 4 red pairs. There is a red passive pair in the Winkie pin footside.

You can choose other colours, but it needs to be chosen quite carefully. Some of the threads from the rose ground also become the passives of the fan. The fan's workers colour the fan, but the passives still tend to show through, and since the passives are different colours, this can be noticeable. I have chosen colours fairly close together.

**Tip:** It is easy to get confused by all the different coloured pairs. In this pattern and the last, every cross-over has different coloured pairs, so this is one way to check that you haven't made a mistake yet! The pin stitches sometimes have both pairs the same colour, and sometimes different, so there's no help there.

## Pattern 5e - Roses and scallops

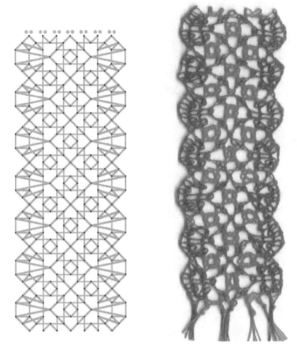

Another technique to colour rose ground is to separate the units of rose ground by lines of Torchon ground. In this pattern, which has 14 pairs, the rose ground units are red, with the Torchon ground and small scallops green.

Be careful about the cross-overs. There are cross-overs both before and after the lines of Torchon ground.

It would also be possible to colour the units of rose ground as in the previous patterns. However, just because you can add more colour, it doesn't necessary mean you should. Think about what the final effect will be. It could end up rather messy.

Since the headsides are scallops, the passives are more visible than in fans.

## Pattern 5f - Roses and diamonds

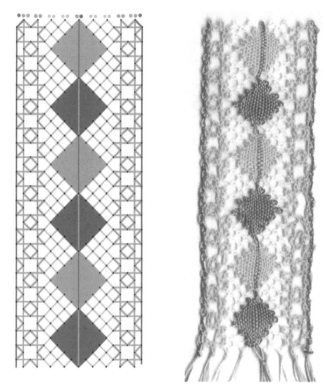

It is possible to have a line of rose ground running down the side of the lace. This makes a strong and attractive edge.

This pattern uses 20 pairs, with one dark green and one pale green pair for the workers of the diamonds (see pattern 3d). The Winkie pin footside passives are dark green, and the rose ground is pale green (4 pairs each side). You could use different colours for these, if you wish.

The rose ground can be a little confusing. Every time the two pairs are the same colour at a pin, work them as Torchon ground (half stitch, pin, half stitch). When they are different colours, work them as double Torchon ground (cloth stitch and twist, pin, cloth stitch and twist). This is necessary to make sure that the rose ground colour stays within the rose ground, and doesn't travel into the Torchon ground. Don't forget the cross-overs! You may spot a mistake in the photo above. In a previous pattern, I left out a cross-over. Here I seem to have left out a whole rose ground unit. I got confused!

# Summary – Rose ground

A unit of rose ground uses 4 pairs of bobbins, 2 on each side. The 2 pairs on the left before the unit end up on the right, and vice versa. That means that if you make each couple of pairs the same colour, and change the colours from one unit to the next, you end up with diagonal crossing double lines, looking a bit like a tartan (see pattern 5a).

If the 2 pairs on one side are different from each other, you can end up with a different style of pattern, as in pattern 5c.

Rose ground is complicated, and these are not the only possible variation. You can use a simple pattern such as pattern 5a, altering which pairs are which colour, and see the result. They do tend to spoil the basic look of the roses, though.

You can separate the rose units with lines of Torchon ground, colouring them differently. This high-lights the roses.

You can have a single line of rose ground down the lace's edge, and this can be coloured as well, if you wish. Remember to use double Torchon ground stitches to "bounce back" the coloured pairs into the rose ground again.

This section covers only one type of rose ground – there are several others, for example using half stitch for cross-overs, or cloth stitch and twist at the pins. If you want to experiment with other rose ground, use pattern 5a with different combinations of coloured pairs and see what happens!

# Spiders

A spider is a simple, large feature, common in Torchon lace. There are different types of spider, but this section only deals with the most common.

This type of spider has a number of pairs (at least two) coming in from the left and the same number of pairs coming in from the right. These are twisted several times, to make the legs of the spider. They work across each other in cloth stitch, a pin is put in the middle of the pairs, then they are worked back again. All pairs are twisted several times again.

A spider may be by itself, surrounded by something to frame it, or several spiders together make a ground.

The pairs which start from the left end up on the left, and vice versa. That sounds dull, but you can produce some interesting patterns.

## Pattern 6a - Spiders separated by Torchon ground

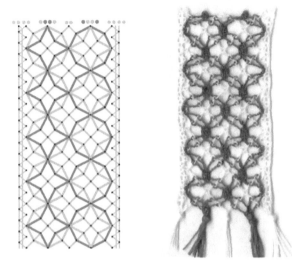

This pattern uses 18 pairs, with 4 red pairs, 4 blue pairs, and 10 pairs of background colour.

These spiders are separated by lines of Torchon ground. The spiders on the left have blue pairs on the outside and red pairs on the inside. The spiders on the right are the opposite way round. The spiders in the middle are more confused!

The effect of the colouring is to create shapes between the spiders, and the spiders themselves merely become the junctions of these shapes.

At the edge of the lace, there are "half spiders". The legs of the spiders (twisted as usual) are joined together by a white pair from the edge working through them in cloth stitch, pin, then working back again.

Remember to twist all coloured pairs several times between stitches.

## Pattern 6b - Spiders as petals and leaves

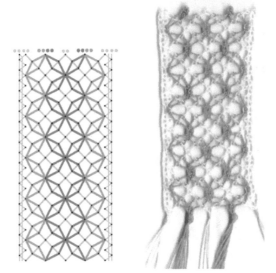

This is exactly the same pattern as pattern 6a, with a different arrangement of coloured pairs, and different colours, pink and green.

This emphasises the spiders more, especially the pink ones in the middle.

I see the pink part as the petals of flowers, with leaves down the edge.

You can try different colours, or different arrangement of the coloured pairs. See what happens!

## Pattern 6c - Spiders next to each other

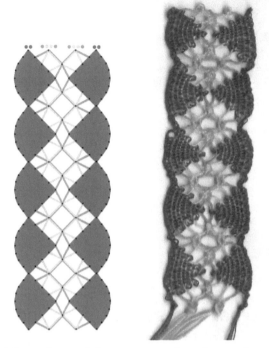

This pattern uses 12 pairs. 4 brown pairs to colour the fans. 4 yellow pairs and 4 orange pairs make the spiders.

Here, the spiders are next to each other, without any line of Torchon ground between. So the two legs going from one spider to the next lie next to each other. This pattern makes these two legs different colours. Round the edge of the ground, where the legs enter or leave the fans, they get spread out again.

This type of ground makes the spiders run together more. The group of four spiders makes a composite shape.

## Pattern 6d - Different sized spiders

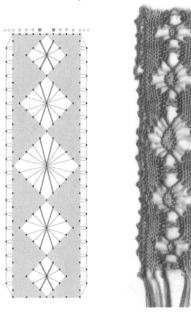

In spiders, the top two pairs cross over, surround the body of the spider, and cross over again to become the bottom two legs. If you have these pairs a different colour to the other pairs in the spider, this makes a feature of the spider's body. It happened in the previous patterns, but it isn't so noticeable for small spiders with 8 legs. So this pattern has 8, 12 and 16 legged spiders to show the different effects.

The pattern uses 14 pairs. There are 2 red pairs that frame the body of the spider. Then there are 6 pale blue pairs which make up the other legs. The remaining 6 dark blue pairs colour the cloth-work, with a worker pair, an edge pair and the footside passive pair. This cloth work is similar to triangles, but they overlap for the smaller spiders. This is easy to work, but you need to tighten the passives well, as some do not necessarily leave the cloth work for some time.

# Summary – Spiders

Spiders have a number of legs (usually 8, 12 or 16) and a body. This count includes the legs above and below the body, which use the same pairs. So an 8 legged spider uses 4 pairs, 2 coming in from the left, and 2 from the right.

The pairs from the left and the pairs from the right cross each other using cloth stitch. A pin is put in the middle, and they cross back again. So the pairs end up in the same order as they started. If you colour the pairs on the left one colour, and the pairs on the right a different colour, the colours will end up on their original sides, which produces an interesting effect (pattern 6b) If the pairs on one side are different from each other, and this is mirrored on the other side, you get a different effect (pattern 6a).

Spider ground can be either spiders next to each other, where legs run side by side, or with lines of Torchon ground between, where the legs get separated.

If you colour the top two legs, these will frame the body of the spider. This works best for spiders with more legs.

# What next?

I hope this book will give you enough confidence to use colour in other lace patterns.

Pattern 1a gives you a strip of Torchon ground which you can use to experiment using colour in Torchon ground. There are bigger grids which you can print off here:

**www.theedkins.co.uk/jo/lace/make.htm**

Pattern 2a is a simple pattern of fans and Torchon ground, and pattern 4a has a similar pattern using scallops. Again, use these to experiment, with cloth stitch or half stitch. Pattern 2d has two headsides of fans touching each other. This book gives lots of patterns using these, but I am sure you can find more. If you want to try using different sized fans, then either adapt one of the patterns in this book, or start from the grids above and make your own.

Once you understand fans, then you can see what you can do with shapes such as diamonds. You might be able to adapt some of the patterns here, but diamonds, zigzags, hearts and triangles are very easy to draw on a blank grid, with footsides either side. Let me tempt you into starting to design your own lace!

Pattern 5a is a simple diamond-shaped area of rose ground. You can use the same idea to try out different colour combinations in rose ground, or other grounds.

Pattern 6a is a simple strip of 8 legged spiders, also suitable for colour experimentation.

If that is too challenging, then you can repeat some of the patterns in this book using different colours. That way you can get several different pieces of lace from one pattern. It's surprising to see what a difference a change of colour makes. See the next section, Colour Theory, for some ideas.

Another approach is adding colour to existing single colour patterns. Have a good look at the pattern and try tracing the threads, imagining them as coloured and think whether it would make an attractive pattern. There are obvious things to look for:

- If there is a footside, then passives in footsides can always be coloured. You may find that dull, as it's just a straight line, but it does frame the lace, especially if it is an insertion with two footsides.
- Headsides give you more opportunities. There is a big section in this book telling you lots of tricks for colour in fans, and they apply equally to scallops. But the simplest effect is the worker pair and edge pair being a different colour to the rest of the lace. This gives a lift to the whole lace. The footside passives could be the same colour.
- Shapes or cloth-work within the lace need more care. Check to see if the cloth-work can share the same pair of workers throughout the lace. This is true if the shapes touch, or there is one zigzag which runs throughout the lace. If so, then you can have a coloured pair of workers, for cloth stitch, or a single coloured thread, for half stitch. Think which colour as well. Make the workers a bold colour if you want to emphasise the shape. But if you use a more neutral colour, and have a bold background colour, then the shape, such as a zigzag, can frame the lace either side of it.
- If the shapes don't touch, then there may be some way to get the worker pair from one shape to the next. If there is Torchon ground between, then the worker pair from one shape can travel through it (possibly with some double Torchon ground where a change of direction is necessary) to get to the next shape. Unfortunately this worker pair will be visible in the ground , but perhaps it can provide an extra feature.
- Other grounds and spiders can a bit tricky to colour. They need a precise combination of coloured pairs to get a

particular coloured effect. They tend to be surrounded by other parts of the lace, and it may not be possible to get the right colours at the start, or to get them out of one part to the start of the next. Still, try tracing the paths of the threads to see what you can do.

These are all controlled ways of colouring lace. You can deliberately make a chaotic colouring. There are multi-coloured threads that can produce attractive (if unpredictable) results.

Don't restrict yourself to simple coloured thread either. There is a wide choice of different types of metallic or iridescent thread. This type of thread can be more expensive or come in small reels, but once you have mastered using colour, you can use just one or two coloured pairs in a pattern, perhaps as workers or footside passives. This is also helpful if you have nearly finished a reel and want to use it up, but don't have enough for every pair in a pattern. A piece of lace made entirely made of gold glittery thread might be a little overwhelming anyway (although I confess I've done that!)

# Colour Theory

The most important point about colour is that you should use the colour or combination of colours that you like. It doesn't matter if they are not supposed to go together. Ignore all that and go for it!

However, colour theory might help you work out why things don't work, or give you ideas to try.

There are two areas: paler/darker and hue (different colours). It is tempting to concentrate on mixing different colours, but dark and pale seem to have an important effect in lace. If you mix several dark colours with pale ones, then the subtleties of the difference between the dark colours may be swamped by a general sense of darkness.

A useful combination is a dark and pale version of the same colour. These provide a bold contrast:

There can be problems if you try three shades of the same colour. It is surprisingly hard to get these evenly spaced. You end up either with two pale colours and one dark, or vice versa.

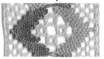

Even with two shades of one colour, they can be too close together to produce the contrast you want, even if they look different on the reels.

How do you know? The only way is to try it and see.

You must remember the dark/pale aspect even when you move onto considering different colours. Some colours are naturally pale, like yellow. Other colours look bright on the reel, but dark in the lace itself. When I wanted fans of red, green and blue, I used dark colours (which were bright colours on the reel).

Adding yellow, I thought it worked better if all the colours were pale.

The human eye seems to adjust for the differences between the shades.

Now to consider mixing different colours. There are colours which are opposite to each other, such as red and green, and yellow and blue. Using these opposite colours can provide a strong contrast.

If you think of a rainbow, the colours are purple, blue, green, yellow, orange, red. You can make this into a circle, so purple is next to red as well. Colours next to each other tend to blend rather than contrasting. This can produce subtle effects, or you can lose colours. This is orange, red and yellow. The orange workers manage to hide the red and yellow fan passives:

You also need to consider what the lace stitch does to the threads. Half stitch tends to show the passives more than cloth stitch. However, cloth stitch doesn't hide them altogether. Here are two versions of the same pattern, one with brown workers on the fans, and yellow and orange passives (which go on to make the spiders). The other version has dark pink and pale blue passives, with pale yellow workers, which end up looking white in the photo:

 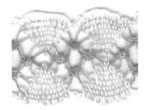

Pale workers can cause problems!

So far, we have dealt with coloured pairs where both threads are the same colour. They don't need to be, of course. Pattern 4d varied between workers of pale pink, pale and dark pink mixed, and dark pink:

I expected the mixed pair to be midway between the dark and pale, but it looks closer to the dark to me. Sigh. That eye readjustment to colour again! Still, combining two different coloured threads in the same pair could be used in any pattern. Try it and see what happens.

One more thing: where you are going to use the lace, and what colours will this involve? You may sew it onto clothes, or a backing fabric. It may be a mat lying on a table. You may glue it to a card. You have to consider the colour of this as well as the colours within the lace. So you could have several colours of headside, the colour of the ground, but also the colour of the backing, which will show through the lace. That is a lot of colours to think about!

# Stitches used in this book

Here is a brief description of the stitches used in this book. For a fuller description, see my book "Bobbin Lace Stitches and Techniques - a reference book of the basics", or visit my website: **www.theedkins.co.uk/jo/lace**

- Cross
- Twist
- Half stitch
- Cloth stitch
- Cloth stitch and twist
- Torchon ground
- Double Torchon ground
- Rose ground
- Spider
- Twisted footside
- Winkie pin footside
- Fan headside
- Scallop headside

# Components of a stitch

**Cross:** Middle two bobbins, left over right.

**Twist:** Two bobbins of a pair, right over left.
Usually both pairs of a stitch are twisted.

# Stitches

**Half stitch:** *Cross, twist both*

**Cloth stitch:** *Cross, twist both, cross*

**Cloth stitch and twist:** *Cross, twist both, cross, twist both*

# Grounds

**Torchon ground:** *Half stitch*, pin, *half stitch*

**Double Torchon ground:** *Cloth stitch and twist,* pin, *cloth stitch and twist*

**Rose ground**
Left two pairs: *Cloth stitch and twist*
Right two pairs: *Cloth stitch and twist*
(New) middle two pairs: *Half stitch,* pin, *half stitch*
(New) left two pairs: *Half stitch,* pin, *half stitch*
(New) right two pairs: *Half stitch,* pin, *half stitch*
(New) middle two pairs: *Half stitch,* pin, *half stitch*
(New) left two pairs: *Cloth stitch and twist*
(New) right two pairs: *Cloth stitch and twist*

# Spider

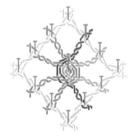

*Twist* all pairs several times. Count pairs from left.
Pair 2 *cloth stitch* with pairs 3 and 4
Pair 1 *cloth stitch* with same pairs
Pin in middle
(New) pair 2 *cloth stitch* with pairs 3 and 4
(New) pair 1 *cloth stitch* with same pairs
*Twist* all pairs several times.

# Footsides

**Twisted footside**

Left two pairs: *Cloth stitch and twist*

(New) right two pairs: *Cloth stitch and twist*

Pin inside both (new) right two pairs

(New) left two pairs: *Cloth stitch, twist both*

**Winkie pin footside:** *Cloth stitch and twist,* pin, *cloth stitch and twist*

# Headsides

Line represents a pair of threads.

**Fan headside** (in cloth or half stitch)
Pairs enter the fan from the right until mid-point, then they leave the fan from the right. The fan is shaped by the gentle curving passives.

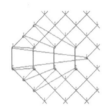

**Scallop headside**
Stitches: *cloth stitch and twist*
Change direction: stitch before and after pin
Pins bordering lace: *half stitch, pin, half stitch*

Made in United States
Troutdale, OR
05/20/2024

20011833R00071